A NEW CHRONOLOGY FOR

THE KINGS OF ISRAEL AND JUDAH

AND ITS IMPLICATIONS FOR

BIBLICAL HISTORY AND LITERATURE

JOHN H. HAYES

AND

PAUL K. HOOKER

John Knox Press
ATLANTA

Biblical quotations are the authors' translations.

Library of Congress Cataloging-in-Publication Data

Hayes, John Haralson, 1934-
   A new chronology for the kings of Israel and
Judah and its implications for Biblical history
and literature.

   1. Bible. O.T.   Kings--Chronology.   7-89
2. Jews--History--953-586, B.C.--Chronology.
I. Hooker, Paul K.   II. Title.
BS1355. 5H39   1988   222'.5095   88-796
ISBN: 0-8042-0152-8

© copyright John Knox Press 1988
10 9 8 7 6 5 4 3 2 1
Printed in the United States of America
John Knox Press
Atlanta, Georgia 30365

c. 1

Contents

Preface 5

Abbreviations 7

1. Chronological Reckoning in Israel and Judah
   and Principles of Interpretation. 9

2. From Jeroboam I to Baasha. 16

3. From Baasha to Zimri. 22

4. From Omri to Jehoram. 25

5. Jehoram and Ahaziah 32

6. From Jehu to Jeroboam II 38

7. From Jeroboam II to Menahem. 50

8. From Menahem to the First Capture of Samaria 57

9. From the Second Capture of Samaria
   to the Rise of Babylonia 68

10. From the Rise of Babylonia to the
    First Capture of Jerusalem 84

11. Zedekiah and Gedaliah 94

12. The Implications of the Present Study 99

Month Names in the Jewish Calendar. 101

Chart of the Israelite and Judean Kings 102

Preface

Through the centuries of biblical study, people have been fascinated with biblical chronology and "the mysterious numbers of the Hebrew kings." No system for dating nor scheme of dates for the Israelite and Judean kings has achieved anything approaching universal acceptance. Contemporary histories of Israel and biblical commentaries currently employ a number of different chronologies.

The chronology for Israelite and Judean kings proposed in the present volume is based on two assumptions. First, an overall consistency must have characterized the calendar and regnal calculations in the two states; otherwise, such calculations would have had little or no value. To argue, as is often done, that the years of a king's reign were simply rounded off, that a single year was assigned to two kings, or that two persons ruled jointly in the same state is to assume that the ancients employed so inconsistent a system of reckoning as to constitute no system at all. For this reason, we also assume that all chronological data provided in 1-2 Kings must be given consideration regardless of whether the data are ultimately utilized in the reconstruction of the chronology or determined to be worthless. The principles involved in ancient Israelite and Judean reckoning of regnal years and dating and the principles we have used in interpreting the biblical data are discussed in the opening section of the book.

Frequently we have noted, in almost propositional form, what we consider the ramifications of and conclusions to be drawn from our chronological reconstructions. These have bearing on numerous historical issues, the dating of prophetic materials, and the literary history of the Old Testament. The conclusions have been stated wherever we considered them to be of interest and are summarized in the final chapter. Many of these will need further discussion and substantiation.

For suggestions and assistance on the present volume, we are indebted to graduate students at Emory University, especially Julie Galambush, Margaret Reeves, and Dean Reed, to Dorcas Doward for the typing, and to the staff of John Knox Press for agreeing to publish the present work without the normal typesetting and proofreading stages. The type was set with Nota Bene, the academic word processing program from Dragonfly Software.

Abbreviations

ABC	*Assyrian and Babylonian Chronicles*, by A. K. Grayson. Locust Valley, NY: J. J. Augustin, 1975
AcOr	*Acta Orientalia*
AEL	*Ancient Egyptian Literature: A Book of Readings*, by Miriam Lichtheim. 3 vols. Berkeley and London: University of California Press, 1973-80
AfO	*Archiv für Orientforschung*
AGS	*Assyrische Gebete an den Sonnengott für Statt und königliches Haus aus der Zeit Asarhaddons und Assurbanipals*, by J. A. Knudtzon. Leipzig: Eduard Pfieffer, 1893
ANET	*Ancient Near Eastern Texts Relating to the Old Testament*, ed. by J. B. Pritchard. 3rd ed. Princeton: Princeton University Press, 1969
Ant	*Jewish Antiquities*, by Josephus
AOAT	*Alter Orient und Altes Testament*
ARAB	*Ancient Records of Assyria and Babylonia*, by D. D. Luckenbill. 2 vols. Chicago: University of Chicago Press, 1926-27
AS	*The Annals of Sennacherib*, by D. D. Luckenbill. Chicago: University of Chicago Press, 1924
AUSS	*Andrews University Seminary Studies*
BA	*Biblical Archaeologist*
BAR	*Biblical Archaeology Reader*
BASOR	*Bulletin of the American Schools of Oriental Research*
BETL	*Bibliotheca Ephemeridum Theologicarum Lovaniensium*
CBQ	*Catholic Biblical Quarterly*
CDP	*Catalogue of the Demotic Papyri in the John Rylands Library*, ed. by F. L. Griffith. 3 vols. Manchester: University Press, 1909
DZGW	*Deutsche Zeitschrift für Geschichtswissenschaft*
EI	*Eretz Israel*
IAKA	*Die Inschriften Asarhaddons Königs von Assyrien*, by R. Borger. Graz: Archiv für Orientforschung, 1956
IDB	*Interpreter's Dictionary of the Bible*

IDBS	*Interpreter's Dictionary of the Bible: Supplementary Volume*
IEJ	*Israel Exploration Journal*
JANES	*Journal of the Ancient Near Eastern Society of Columbia University*
JAOS	*Journal of the American Oriental Society*
JARCE	*Journal of the American Research Center in Egypt*
JBL	*Journal of Biblical Literature*
JCS	*Journal of Cuneiform Studies*
JDT	*Jahrbücher für deutsche Theologie*
JNES	*Journal of Near Eastern Studies*
JQR	*Jewish Quarterly Review*
Or	*Orientalia*
OTS	*Oudtestamentische Studiën*
PEQ	*Palestine Exploration Quarterly*
SAK	*Studien zur altägyptische Kultur*
SDB	*Supplements Dictionaire Biblique*
SH	*Scripta Hierosolymitana*
ST	*Studia Theologica*
SVT	*Supplements to Vetus Testamentum*
TA	*Tel Aviv*
TSBA	*Transactions of the Society of Biblical Archaeology*
VT	*Vetus Testamentum*
WHJP	*World History of the Jewish People*
WO	*Welt des Orient*
ZAW	*Zeitschrift für die alttestamentliche Wissenschaft*
ZDMG	*Zeitschrift der deutschen morgenländischen Gesellschaft*
ZDPV	*Zeitschrift des deutschen Palästina-Vereins*

1. Chronological Reckoning in Israel and Judah and Principles of Interpretation

W. F. **Albright**, "The Chronology of the Divided Monarchy of Israel," *BASOR* 100(1945)16-22; **Albright**, "Prolegomenon" to the reissue of C. F. **Burney**, *The Book of Judges with Introduction and Notes on the Hebrew Text of the Books of Kings* (New York: Ktav, 1970)1-38; K. T. **Andersen**, "Die Chronologie der Könige von Israel und Juda," *ST* 23(1969)69-114; W. H. **Barnes**, *Studies in the Chronology of the Divided Monarchy of Israel* (dissertation, Harvard University, 1986); J. **Begrich**, *Die Chronologie der Könige von Israel und Juda und die Quellen des Rahmens der Königsbücher* (Tübingen: J. C. B. Mohr [Paul Siebeck], 1929); V. **Coucke**, "Chronologie Biblique," *SDB* 1(1928)1244-79; S. J. **De Vries**, "Chronology of the OT," *IDB* 1(1962)580-99; **De Vries**, "Chronology, OT," *IDBS* (1976)161-66; J. **Finegan**, *Handbook of Biblical Chronology: Principles of Time Reckoning in the Ancient World and Problems of Chronology in the Bible* (Princeton: Princeton University Press, 1964); D. N. **Freedman**, "The Chronology of Israel and the Ancient Near East," *The Bible and the Ancient Near East* (ed. G. E. Wright; Garden City: Doubleday & Company, 1961)203-14; A. **Hellemann**, *Chronologia probabiliter vera historiae Judaicae et Israeliticae gentis ab Abrahamo ad Christum computata* (Hafniae: Officina "Athene," 1925); F. A. **Herzog**, *Die Chronologie der beiden Königsbücher* (Münster: Aschendorffsche Verlagsbuchhandlung, 1909); J. R. A. **Hughes**, *Secrets of the Times: The Chronology of the Hebrew Bible* (Sheffield: JSOT Press, 1988); A. **Jepsen**, "Ein neuer Fixpunkt für die Chronologie der israelitischen Könige?," *VT* 20(1970)359-61; A. **Jepsen** and R. **Hanhart**, *Untersuchungen zur israelitisch-jüdischen Chronologie* (Berlin: Alfred Töpelmann, 1964); A. **Kamphausen**, *Die Chronologie der hebräischen Könige: Eine geschichtlich Untersuchung* (Bonn: Max Cohen & Sohn, 1883); F. X. **Kugler**, *Von Moses bis Paulus* (Münster: Aschendorffsche Verlagsbuchhandlung, 1922)136-50; C. **Lederer**, *Die biblische Zeitrechnung vom Auszuge aus Ägypten bis zum Beginne der Babylonischen Gefangenschaft* (Speier: Ferd. Eleeberger, 1888); J. **Lewy**, *Die Chronologie der Könige von Israel und Juda* (Giessen: Alfred Töpelmann, 1927); J. M. **Miller**, "Another Look at the Chronology of the Early Divided Monarchy," *JBL* 86(1967)276-88; S. **Mowinckel**, "Die Chronologie der israelitischen und judäischen Könige," *AcOr* 10(1932)161-277; A. **Murtonen**, "On the Chronology of the Old Testament," *ST* 8(1954)133-37; V. **Pavlovský** and E. **Vogt**, "Die Jahre der Könige von Juda und Israel," *Biblica* 45(1964)321-47; J. **Reade**, "Mesopotamian Guidelines for Biblical Chronology," *Syro-Mesopotamian Studies* 4/1(1981)1-9; R. **Rühl**, "Chronologie der Könige von Israel und Juda," *DZGW* 12(1894-95)44-76, 171; C. **Shedl**, "Textkritische Bemerkungen zu den Sychronismen der Könige von Israel und Juda," *VT* 12(1962)88-119; J. D. **Shenkel**, *Chronology and Recensional Development in the Greek Text of Kings* (Cambridge: Harvard University Press, 1968); M. **Stiles**, Shophar: *Synchronizing Hebrew Originals from Available Records* (Aptos, CA: Self-published, 1972-   ); H. **Tadmor**, "The Chronology of the First Temple Period: A Presentation and Evaluation of the Sources," *WHJP* 4/1(1979)44-60, 318-320 = J. A. Soggin, *A History of Ancient Israel* (London/Philadelphia: SCM Press/Westminster Press, 1984)368-83, 408-11; S. **Talmon**, "Divergencies in Calendar-Reckoning in Ephraim and Judah," *VT* 8(1958)48-74; E. R. **Thiele**, *The Mysterious Numbers of the Hebrew Kings: A Reconstruction of the Chronology of the Kingdoms of Israel and Judah* (3rd ed.; Grand Rapids: Zondervan, 1984); M. **Vogelstein**, *Fertile Soil: A Political History Under the Divided Monarchy* (New York: American Press, 1957); J. **Wellhausen**, "Die Zeitrechnung des Buchs der Könige seit der Theilung des Reichs," *JDT* 20(1875)607-40; W. R. **Wifall**, Jr., "The Chronology of the Divided Monarchy of Israel," *ZAW* 80(1968)319-37.

The books of Kings provide three types of chronological information about Israelite and Judean kings. One form of information is provided by statements on the length of reigns of each individual Israelite and Judean ruler. Such information is supplied for every monarch except Queen Athaliah of Judah (2 Kings 11). A second type of information is contained in the synchronisms in which the beginning of a Judean ruler's reign is correlated with the year of an Israelite ruler's reign and vice versa. Such synchronisms are provided for all rulers except those who assumed the throne in the same year, namely Rehoboam and Jeroboam I and Athaliah and Jehu. A third type of information is provided in the occasional correlation of events in biblical history with the years of non-biblical monarchs.

As has long been noted, this chronological information is frequently problematic and even contradictory. Synchronisms sometimes clash with one another. Some synchronisms do not correlate with the data given about the length of reigns. The length of reigns supplied between two points common to the histories of both nations frequently do not total the same number of years.

Some scholars have assumed that the chronological information supplied for the Israelite and Judean kings forms part of a non-historical, schematic chronology extending from Genesis through Second Kings and as such has been adjusted or produced to fit this larger overarching scheme. Such an approach despairs of any attempt to establish dates and correlations for biblical rulers except in a very general sense.

Approaches which take the biblical data as reasonably reflective of actual chronological realities have attempted to solve the various problems involved in one of five different ways or through a combination of these. (1) Some scholars assume a number of errors and corruptions in the text and thus resort to various forms of textual corrections. The weakness of such an approach is its need to correct the Hebrew text often without any manuscript or versional support. (2) Another approach draws upon the evidence of ancient translations or recensions, especially the Lucianic (or proto-Lucianic) recension of the Greek translation, where these differ from the standard Hebrew text. Such utilization of evidence drawn from translations, however, is employed very selectively and only with regard to the reigns of certain kings. (3) Some scholars assume that the length of reigns assigned kings was rounded off so that the years are occasionally approximate rather than exact. A chronological reconstruction based on such an assumption could never be more than approximate. (4) Other approaches assume that different systems for counting a monarch's years were employed at different times in both Israel and Judah. Under such a system, the same year was frequently assigned to two different rulers, but at only times not. Recourse to such a diversity in reckoning is based on the need to make synchronisms work rather than on any susbstantial evidence indicating such shifts. (5) Most modern chronologies assume a number of co-regencies when two kings ruled jointly over the same kingdom with the years of a co-regency being assigned to both kings. The weakness of this assumption is the fact that the hypothesis of co-regencies is without biblical warrant.

No chronological system has or is able to accept as historically accurate all the chronological data in the books of Kings. Our proposed chronology is based on a number of assumptions and conclusions about the nature of chronological reckoning in ancient Israel and Judah and about the nature of the biblical evidence. We have summarized these in the following fifteen paragraphs.

(1) The primary reason for numbering the years of a king's reign was dating contractual agreements and government business. In addition to governmental edicts and orders, time-conditioned private contracts, such as loans and leases and agreements of indentured servitude, would have been dated generally with reference to the day and month of a particular year of a king's reign although only year dates may have been used even without the king's name, as in the Samaria ostraca.

(2) There were no co-regencies, periods when two monarchs ruled jointly, in either Israel or Judah. The two cases in which there appears to have been joint rulership--Solomon with David (1 Kings 1:38-40; 2:10-12) and Jotham with Azariah (2 Kings 15:5)--were, in fact, not co-regencies. Solomon was apparently anointed and installed as king before the death of David and thus was monarch in his own right. David plays no significant role in the narratives after Solomon's assumption of power. Jotham is said to have functioned for a time in a prominent role as the one "over the household, governing the people of the land" (2 Kings 15:5) during the reign of Azariah, but his office during this brief period until he became king is clearly specified and did not constitute monarchical rule.

(3) Five kings--Baasha in Israel and Asa, Jehoash, Amaziah, and Azariah in Judah--either abdicated voluntarily because of illness and physical problems or were forced to give up the throne, and consequently were succeeded by new kings. Except in the case of Baasha, biblical evidence indicates the reason for the surrender or loss of the throne. Certain physical ailments would have rendered the king unclean and/or incompetent, thus making his participation in cultic affairs impossible and, in turn, his abdication mandatory.

(4) The numbering of the years of a king's reign, until the calendar change in the eighteenth year of Josiah (see 11 below), was always from the fall new year festival. Year 1 began with the anointment and coronation at the autumn celebration; year 2 at the second fall festival of a king's reign, and so on.

(5) The years assigned a king were counted from the first autumn festival of his reign until his death. Generally, a king ruled until his death, but in the case of abdications the years a king lived

after abdication were numbered as part of his reign. The years from the time he began to reign could continue to be used to specify the date of an event, agreement, or contract even though he was no longer the reigning monarch. King Hoshea's years continued to be employed for dating events, for example, even after he was imprisoned by the Assyrians (2 Kings 17:1-6).

(6) On three occasions, because of special historical and political circumstances, no king was on the throne at the new year festival. The three cases involved the Zechariah-Shallum-Menahem struggle, the Jehoahaz II-Jehoiakim transition following the death of Josiah at Megiddo, and the Jehoiachin-Zedekiah succession following the first capture of Jerusalem by the Babylonians. The years involved (747-746, 609-608, and 597-596) were thus not attributed to any king.

(7) Point 4 above means that ante-dating, or crediting the partial accession year to a new king, was never practiced in either Israel or Judah. A new king began to rule upon the death or abdication of the former king and may have ruled the greater part of a year before the next new year festival. This period, however, was attributed to the preceding ruler on the throne at the last new year festival.

(8) If a king was on the throne at the new year festival, he was assigned a year's reign regardless of the length of his rule. Conversely, a king who ruled but was not on the throne at any regnal festival celebration was never assigned a year's rule. The latter was the case with Zimri, Zechariah, Shallum, Jehoahaz II, and Jehoiachin.

(9) The new year festival was observed in what came to be the seventh month in Judah and the eighth month in Israel. Throughout its history, the northern kingdom of Israel observed a Marheshvan to Marheshvan calendar, while Judah employed a Tishri to Tishri calendar until the eighteenth year of Josiah.

(10) The "day of the king" (Hos. 7:5)--and the beginning of a new (regnal) year--was observed as a major celebration during the autumn festival. This took place on the fifteenth of the eighth month in Israel and of the seventh month in Judah (before the calendar change under Josiah). In early monarchical times, the celebration of the fall festival was apparently a three-day affair (see Exod. 19:10-11; Hos. 6:2; Amos 4:4b) during which the first two days would have paralleled the later rituals of Rosh Hashanah and Yom Kippur. The "day of the king" and the annual celebration of the enthronement of Yahweh would have been observed on the third day.

(11) One major calendar change occurred in pre-exilic Judean history. During the eighteenth year of Josiah's reign, the Judeans

shifted from an autumn to a spring calendar, making Nisan the first
month of the year and thus the reference point for the calculation of
the years of a monarch's rule. Josiah's eighteenth year was eighteen
months long, extending from Tishri 624 to Nisan 622. All subsequent dates in 2 Kings as well as in the books of Jeremiah and
Ezekiel are calculated on the basis of a Nisan to Nisan year. This
change in the calendar provides a pivotal point for dating the literary
strata of the Pentateuch.

(12) The regnal years assigned the kings are essentially
trustworthy, although three factors complicate matters even with
regard to the regnal periods. (a) Three Israelite kings have been
assigned more regnal years than they actually ruled--Omri twelve
years instead of eleven, Ahab twenty-two years instead of fifteen,
and Jehu twenty-eight years instead of eighteen. The reasons for
these will be discussed below. (b) The practice of continuing to number the years of a king's reign even after his abdication has created
some confusion. The final editors of the Kings material assumed
that the years attributed to a king were years he actually ruled before
the next king succeeded to the throne. Several synchronisms made
on this basis are clearly incorrect. (c) Pekah's reign of twenty years
included sixteen years during which he was a rival king in the north
(from 750 until 734). The attempt to place all twenty years of his
reign into the period following his takeover in Samaria in 734 (after
Tishri 734, the beginning of Azariah's fifty-second year [see 2 Kings
15:27]), again introduced confusion into the efforts at editorial synchronization.

(13) As a rule, the synchronisms for the accession of Israelite
and Judean monarchs were made on the basis of reference to the
current ruler of the other state. That is, the beginning of a king's
reign in Judah was synchronized with that of an Israelite king and
vice versa. There appear to have been two cases that were excep-
tions to that practice. The synchronisms for the beginning of the
reigns of Jehoahaz and Jehoash of Israel (2 Kings 13:1, 10) seem
originally to have been recorded in terms of Hazael's reign in
Damascus, but giving only the year number without the Syrian
ruler's name. The editors of the biblical traditions assumed that the
year references were to Jehoash of Judah.

(14) Since the biblical material provides evidence only for
establishing the relative relationships and synchronisms between
Israelite and Judean kings, the assignment of specific dates to

Israelite and Judean kings must be based on appeal to external evidence, namely, Assyrian and Babylonian texts. Only one absolute day, month, and year can be established from these sources, namely, the capture of Jerusalem by Nebuchadrezzar on 16 March 597. Other dates can be established with relative certainty, generally to within a year.

(15) In later translations and translation revisions, efforts were made to correct and harmonize the conflicting evidence of the Masoretic text. None of the versions, however, preserves any authentic data that can be employed in reconstructing the chronology. The data contained in the versions are based on efforts to correct the Masoretic text rather than on the use of information independent of the Masoretic text.

2. FROM JEROBOAM I TO BAASHA

JUDAH

REHOBOAM (926-910)
0. . . . . - Tishri 926
1. Tishri 926 - Tishri 925
2. Tishri 925 - Tishri 924
3. Tishri 924 - Tishri 923
4. Tishri 923 - Tishri 922
5. Tishri 922 - Tishri 921
6. Tishri 921 - Tishri 920
7. Tishri 920 - Tishri 919
8. Tishri 919 - Tishri 918
9. Tishri 918 - Tishri 917
10. Tishri 917 - Tishri 916
11. Tishri 916 - Tishri 915
12. Tishri 915 - Tishri 914
13. Tishri 914 - Tishri 913
14. Tishri 913 - Tishri 912
15. Tishri 912 - Tishri 911
16. Tishri 911 - Tishri 910
17. Tishri 910 - . . . .

ABIJAH/ABIJAM (909-907)
0. . . . . - Tishri 909
1. Tishri 909 - Tishri 908
2. Tishri 908 - Tishri 907
3. Tishri 907 - . . . .

ASA (906-878[866])
0. . . . . - Tishri 906
1. Tishri 906 - Tishri 905

2. Tishri 905 - Tishri 904
3. Tishri 904 - Tishri 903

ISRAEL

JEROBOAM I (927-906)
0. . . . . - Marheshvan 927
1. Marheshvan 927 - Marheshvan 926
2. Marheshvan 926 - Marheshvan 925
3. Marheshvan 925 - Marheshvan 924
4. Marheshvan 924 - Marheshvan 923
5. Marheshvan 923 - Marheshvan 922
6. Marheshvan 922 - Marheshvan 921
7. Marheshvan 921 - Marheshvan 920
8. Marheshvan 920 - Marheshvan 919
9. Marheshvan 919 - Marheshvan 918
10. Marheshvan 918 - Marheshvan 917
11. Marheshvan 917 - Marheshvan 916
12. Marheshvan 916 - Marheshvan 915
13. Marheshvan 915 - Marheshvan 914
14. Marheshvan 914 - Marheshvan 913
15. Marheshvan 913 - Marheshvan 912
16. Marheshvan 912 - Marheshvan 911
17. Marheshvan 911 - Marheshvan 910
18. Marheshvan 910 - Marheshvan 909

19. Marheshvan 909 - Marheshvan 908
20. Marheshvan 908 - Marheshvan 907

21. Marheshvan 907 - Marheshvan 906
22. Marheshvan 906 - . . . .

NADAB (905-904)
0. . . . . - Marheshvan 905
1. Marheshvan 905 - Marheshvan 904
2. Marheshvan 904 - . . . .

2. From Jeroboam I to Baasha

W. F. **Albright**, "New Light from Egypt on the Chronology and History of Israel and Judah," *BASOR* 130(1953)4-11; K. **Baer**, "The Libyan and Nubian Kings of Egypt: Notes on the Chronology of Dynasties XXII to XXVI," *JNES* 32(1973)4-25; W. H. **Barnes**, *Studies in the Chronology of the Divided Monarchy of Israel* (dissertation, Harvard University, 1986)70-89; D. J. A. **Clines**, "The Evidence for an Autumnal New Year in Pre-exilic Israel Reconsidered," *JBL* 93(1974)22-40; E. **Danelius**, "The Sins of Jeroboam Ben-Nabat," *JQR* 58(1967-68)95-114, 204-23; D. W. **Gooding**, "The Septuagint's Rival Versions of Jeroboam's Rise to Power," *VT* 17(1967)173-89; R. P. **Gordon**, "The Second Septuagint Account of Jeroboam: History or Midrash?," *VT* 25(1975)368-93; S. **Herrmann**, "Operationen Pharao Schoschenks I. im östlichen Ephraim," *ZDPV* 80(1964)55-79; K. A. **Kitchen**, *The Third Intermediate Period in Egypt (1100-650 B.C.)* (Warminster: Aris & Phillips, 1973); B. **Mazar**, "The Campaign of Pharaoh Shishak to Palestine," *SVT* 4(1957)57-66; M. **Noth**, "Die Wege der Pharaonenheere in Palästina und Syrien. IV. Die Schoschenkenliste," *ZDPV* 61(1938)277-304; J. B. **Segal**, "Intercalation and the Hebrew Calendar," *VT* 7(1957)250-307; S. **Talmon**, "Divergences in Calendar-Reckoning in Ephraim and Judah," *VT* 8(1958)48-74; E. **Vogt**, "Expeditio Pharaonis Shoshenq in Palaestinam A. 927 A. C.," *Biblica* 38(1957)234-36.

Three matters in the chart for this period require preliminary discussion. First, we have employed the later traditional names for the seventh and eighth months and throughout will refer to them by this numbering. In the early monarchical period, these months bore the names Ethanim and Bul, respectively (see 1 Kings 6:38; 8:2). The numbering of the months with the year beginning in the spring, indicated by the explanatory notes (glosses?) in 1 Kings 6:38 and 8:2, was itself a late development (see below, section 10).

Second, calendar reckoning in early Israel and Judah was based on an autumn to autumn year. Royal festivals, regnal anniversaries, and the tabulation of regnal years were associated with the great fall festival (*'asiph* Ingathering) that marked the end or the turning of the year (Exod. 23:16b; 34:22b). Although the oldest cultic lists of festivals enumerate the festivals beginning in spring, this does not imply a spring to spring year since these lists (Exod. 23:14-17; 34:18-23; Deut. 16:1-17) reflect the cycle of harvests, not calendrical concerns. With the new regnal year beginning on the final day of the fall festival, any enumeration of the harvest and festival seasons would have moved from spring to autumn. The fall festival was observed a month later in the north than in the south (compare 1 Kings 8:2 and 12:32) because of agricultural differences: crops matured earlier in the south than in the north. 1 Kings 12:32-33 indicates the fifteenth of the month as the high point of the festival. No specific date nor length of the festival is noted in Exod. 23:16b and 34:22b, which could imply that the time for the celebration may have been determined by actual agricultural conditions. These conditions, however, would not have varied much from year to year since the summer and fall harvests and the subsequent ingathering were not as variable as the spring cereal harvest when the ripening of the grain was determined by variations in the annual rainfall patterns. The length of the fall festival was probably originally three days (see Exod. 19:10-16; Hos. 6:1-2; Amos 4:4b), climaxing on the fifteenth of the month (see Ps. 81:3).

Third, the determination of the years 927 and 926 for the first regnal years of Jeroboam I and Rehoboam is based on calculating backward from later kings' reigns which can be determined with reasonable exactitude. The only noted external contact between these kings and other rulers was the campaign of Shishak (Sheshonq I) into Palestine in the fifth year of Rehoboam (1 Kings 14:25). Although Shishak recorded his invasion on the south wall of the temple at Karnak, his description does not specify a date. Even the years of Shishak's reign are somewhat uncertain, as are those for all the XXIInd Dynasty (from Sheshonq I through Osorkon IV, about 945-712). Of the projected 233 years of this dynasty only about 207 years can be confidently attributed to known monarchs. If one assigns Shishak even the rather high dates of 945 to 924 with potential for three or four years' variance, then he could have conducted a Palestinian campaign in Rehoboam's fifth year (922-921).

Upon the death of Solomon, Rehoboam acceded to the throne and began his exercise of royal authority (1 Kings 11:43). Although nothing is said in Kings about the role of anointment in his assumption of power, one could presume on the basis of a surface reading of other texts that anointment might have occurred immediately after Solomon died, probably just after Tishri 927. The accounts of the anointments of David (2 Sam. 2:4; 5:3), Solomon (1 Kings 1:38-40), and Absalom (2 Sam. 15:7-12; 19:8b-10), and the more legendary material about Saul (1 Sam. 10:1), Jehu (2 Kings 9:1-7), and David (1 Sam. 16:1-13) could imply that anointment might take place anytime. There is, however, no reason not to assume that, of these accounts of anointments, those which actually took place did so at the time of the fall festival. The "day of the king" would thus have been the day of the king's anointment (and its anniversary celebration), the time when the king was ritually declared "sacred" and through the anointment "transferred" to the realm of the holy (see Lev. 8:10-12, 30). Anointment rendered the king sacrosanct (see 1 Sam. 24:6; 26:11) and gave him access to the altar for the performance of at least certain sacrifices, namely, burnt offerings (the *'olah*) and well-being sacrifices (the *zebach shelamim*; see 1 Sam. 6:17; 15:12; 1 Kings 9:25; 12:32-33) if not the right to function as high priest on festival occasions.

First Kings 12:1 states that Rehoboam went to Shechem to be made king (for the anointment and installation service). Whether this text is to be understood with reference to a unique occasion (the king went to Shechem on this occasion to be anointed since the time of the fall festival had already passed in the south) or to a customary observance (the king annually participated in a northern regnal celebration at the fall festival) remains uncertain. 1 Kings 3:3-14 could be understood as indicating the Davidic king's presence at an annual observance of the fall festival at a northern sanctuary. At any rate, Rehoboam had begun to rule in the south but had not yet been anointed and installed, the purpose for which "all Israel" (Israel and Judah) had assembled at Shechem.

The rebellion of the north led to Rehoboam's failure to be anointed in 927 and resulted instead in the anointment and installation of Jeroboam I. The exact details of Jeroboam's rise to kingship and the events surrounding his coronation cannot be established. Different versions, with differing details, have been preserved (1 Kings 12:25-33 in the Masoretic text with 12:24a-z added in the Greek).

Rehoboam was anointed king in Jerusalem at the next fall festival (15 Tishri 726). He reigned for seventeen years (1 Kings 14:21) and was succeeded at his death by Abijah (Abijam) in the eighteenth year of Jeroboam I (15 Tishri 909; 1 Kings 15:1).

Abijah's reign was short lived, only three years. Upon his death, after 15 Tishri 907, he was succeeded by Asa (before 15 Marheshvan 907), just prior to the end of the twentieth year of Jeroboam I (1 Kings 15:9).

Nadab succeeded Jeroboam I in the second year of Asa (1 Kings 15:25) but was assassinated along with the other members of Jeroboam's family by Baasha.

3. FROM BAASHA TO ZIMRI

	JUDAH				ISRAEL

JUDAH

ISRAEL

ASA (906-878[866])

3.	Tishri 904 - Tishri 903
4.	Tishri 903 - Tishri 902
5.	Tishri 902 - Tishri 901
6.	Tishri 901 - Tishri 900
7.	Tishri 900 - Tishri 899
8.	Tishri 899 - Tishri 898
9.	Tishri 898 - Tishri 897
10.	Tishri 897 - Tishri 896
11.	Tishri 896 - Tishri 895
12.	Tishri 895 - Tishri 894
13.	Tishri 894 - Tishri 893
14.	Tishri 893 - Tishri 892
15.	Tishri 892 - Tishri 891
16.	Tishri 891 - Tishri 890
17.	Tishri 890 - Tishri 889
18.	Tishri 889 - Tishri 888
19.	Tishri 888 - Tishri 887
20.	Tishri 887 - Tishri 886
21.	Tishri 886 - Tishri 885
22.	Tishri 885 - Tishri 884
23.	Tishri 884 - Tishri 883
24.	Tishri 883 - Tishri 882
25.	Tishri 882 - Tishri 881

BAASHA (903-882[880])

0.	.... - Marheshvan 903
1.	Marheshvan 903 - Marheshvan 902
2.	Marheshvan 902 - Marheshvan 901
3.	Marheshvan 901 - Marheshvan 900
4.	Marheshvan 900 - Marheshvan 899
5.	Marheshvan 899 - Marheshvan 898
6.	Marheshvan 898 - Marheshvan 897
7.	Marheshvan 897 - Marheshvan 896
8.	Marheshvan 896 - Marheshvan 895
9.	Marheshvan 895 - Marheshvan 894
10.	Marheshvan 894 - Marheshvan 893
11.	Marheshvan 893 - Marheshvan 892
12.	Marheshvan 892 - Marheshvan 891
13.	Marheshvan 891 - Marheshvan 890
14.	Marheshvan 890 - Marheshvan 889
15.	Marheshvan 889 - Marheshvan 888
16.	Marheshvan 888 - Marheshvan 887
17.	Marheshvan 887 - Marheshvan 886
18.	Marheshvan 886 - Marheshvan 885
19.	Marheshvan 885 - Marheshvan 884
20.	Marheshvan 884 - Marheshvan 883
21.	Marheshvan 883 - Marheshvan 882
22.	Marheshvan 882 - ....

ELAH (881-880)

	JUDAH	(Baasha)		ISRAEL
			0.	.... - Marheshvan 881
26.	Tishri 881 - Tishri 880	(23)	1.	Marheshvan 881 - Marheshvan 880
27.	Tishri 880 - Tishri 879	(24)	2.	Marheshvan 880 - ....

ZIMRI (seven days)

3. From Baasha to Zimri

According to 1 Kings 15:27 and 33, Baasha exterminated the house of Jeroboam and began to rule in the third year of Asa after Nadab's two-year rule, begun in the second year of Asa (1 Kings 15:25). The assassination of Nadab thus would have occurred after 15 Marheshvan 904 (the beginning of Nadab's second year) and before 15 Tishri 903 (the beginning of Asa's fourth year).

According to our reconstruction, Baasha abdicated the throne in his twenty-second year (before 15 Marheshvan 881) but continued to live for two additional years, the basis of his assignment of twenty-four years (1 Kings 15:33). No reason for his abdication is hinted at in the text. His abdication is suggested by two factors. (1) His successor, Elah, assumed the throne in the twenty-sixth year of Asa (1 Kings 16:8) which began 15 Tishri 881. This means that Baasha abdicated the throne between 15 Tishri and 15 Marheshvan 881 with Elah being anointed king on the latter date. (2) In references to the assassination of Elah by Zimri (1 Kings 16:3, 7, 8-13), the text makes it clear that Zimri exterminated "Baasha and his house." If Baasha were already dead, such a reference would be unnecessary.

Elah's reign of two years would have begun 15 Marheshvan 881 (in Asa's twenty-sixth year) and his assassination have taken place before 15 Tishri 879 (the beginning of Asa's twenty-eighth year; 1 Kings 16:10). Zimri then reigned for seven days in the twenty-seventh year of Asa (1 Kings 16:15).

4. FROM OMRI TO JEHORAM

JUDAH	ISRAEL

ASA (906-878[866])

27.	Tishri 880 - Tishri 879
28.	Tishri 879 - Tishri 878
29.	Tishri 878 - ....

OMRI (879-869)

0.	.... - Marheshvan 879
1.	Marheshvan 879 - Marheshvan 878
2.	Marheshvan 878 - Marheshvan 877

JEHOSHAPHAT (877-853)

		(Asa)
0.	.... - Tishri 877	
1.	Tishri 877 - Tishri 876	(30)
2.	Tishri 876 - Tishri 875	(31)
3.	Tishri 875 - Tishri 874	(32)
4.	Tishri 874 - Tishri 873	(33)
5.	Tishri 873 - Tishri 872	(34)
6.	Tishri 872 - Tishri 871	(35)
7.	Tishri 871 - Tishri 870	(36)
8.	Tishri 870 - Tishri 869	(37)
9.	Tishri 869 - Tishri 868	(38)

3.	Marheshvan 877 - Marheshvan 876
4.	Marheshvan 876 - Marheshvan 875
5.	Marheshvan 875 - Marheshvan 874
6.	Marheshvan 874 - Marheshvan 873
7.	Marheshvan 873 - Marheshvan 872
8.	Marheshvan 872 - Marheshvan 871
9.	Marheshvan 871 - Marheshvan 870
10.	Marheshvan 870 - Marheshvan 869
11.	Marheshvan 869 - ....

AHAB (868-854)

0.	.... - Marheshvan 868
1.	Marheshvan 868 - Marheshvan 867
2.	Marheshvan 867 - Marheshvan 866
3.	Marheshvan 866 - Marheshvan 865
4.	Marheshvan 865 - Marheshvan 864

10.	Tishri 868 - Tishri 867	(39)
11.	Tishri 867 - Tishri 866	(40)
12.	Tishri 866 - Tishri 865	(41)
13.	Tishri 865 - Tishri 864	

14. Tishri 864 - Tishri 863
15. Tishri 863 - Tishri 862
16. Tishri 862 - Tishri 861
17. Tishri 861 - Tishri 860
18. Tishri 860 - Tishri 859
19. Tishri 859 - Tishri 858
20. Tishri 858 - Tishri 857
21. Tishri 857 - Tishri 856
22. Tishri 856 - Tishri 855
23. Tishri 855 - Tishri 854
24. Tishri 854 - Tishri 853

25. Tishri 853 - ....

JEHORAM (852-841)
0. .... - Tishri 852
1. Tishri 852 - Tishri 851

5. Marheshvan 864 - Marheshvan 863
6. Marheshvan 863 - Marheshvan 862
7. Marheshvan 862 - Marheshvan 861
8. Marheshvan 861 - Marheshvan 860
9. Marheshvan 860 - Marheshvan 859
10. Marheshvan 859 - Marheshvan 858
11. Marheshvan 858 - Marheshvan 857
12. Marheshvan 857 - Marheshvan 856
13. Marheshvan 856 - Marheshvan 855
14. Marheshvan 855 - Marheshvan 854
15. Marheshvan 854 - ....

AHAZIAH (853-852)
0. .... - Marheshvan 853
1. Marheshvan 853 - Marheshvan 852

2. Marheshvan 852 - ....

ASSYRIA
SHALMANESER III (858-824)

0. .... - Nisan 858
1. Nisan 858 - Nisan 857
2. Nisan 857 - Nisan 856
3. Nisan 856 - Nisan 855
4. Nisan 855 - Nisan 854
5. Nisan 854 - Nisan 853

6. Nisan 853 - Nisan 852

7. Nisan 852 - Nisan 851

4. From Omri to Jehoram

F. M. **Cross**, "The Stele Dedicated to Melcarth by Ben-Hadad of Damascus," *BASOR* 205(1972)36-42; M. **Elat**, "The Campaigns of Shalmaneser III Against Aram and Israel," *IEJ* 25(1975)25-35; E. **Lipiński**, "Le Ben-Hadad II de la Bible et l'histoire," *Fifth World Congress of Jewish Studies I* (Jerusalem: World Union of Jewish Studies, 1969)157-73; J. M. **Miller**, "The Elisha Cycle and the Accounts of the Omride Wars," *JBL* 85(1966)441-54; **Miller**, "So Tibni Died (1 Kings xvi 22)," *VT* 18(1968)392-94; W. H. **Shea**, "The Kings of the Melqart Stele," *Maarav* 1(1978-79)159-76; S. **Timm**, *Die Dynastie Omri. Quellen und Untersuchungen zur Geschichte Israels im 9. Jahrhundert vor Christus* (Göttingen: Vandenhoeck & Ruprecht, 1982); C. F. **Whitley**, "The Deuteronomic Presentation of the House of Omri," *VT* 2(1952)137-52.

Upon receipt of the news that Zimri had assassinated Elah and exterminated the house of Baasha, the Israelite army, fighting the Philistines at Gibbethon, immediately proclaimed as king their commander Omri. Zimri, besieged in Tirzah by Omri and the Israelite army, burned the citadel of the palace, and died in its flames (1 Kings 16:15-18). Omri apparently assumed the kingship immediately and was subsequently anointed, on 15 Marheshvan 879. Although no accession formula survives with regard to his replacement of Zimri on the throne, his accession appears, like Zimri's revolt, to have taken place in Asa's twenty-seventh year (before Tishri 879; 1 Kings 16:15).

Omri was forced to fight a civil war with Tibni, an alternate claimant to the throne, which lasted until the thirty-first year of Asa (1 Kings 16:21-23a). Tibni is never spoken of as king in the biblical text although half the population is said to have desired to make him king (1 Kings 16:21). No regnal years are assigned him nor is there any reason to assume that any were ever attributed to him. In the thirty-first year of Asa (876-875), Tibni died and Omri began to rule over the whole of Israel (1 Kings 16:23a).

Omri is said to have ruled for twelve years (1 Kings 16:23a). He was succeeded by Ahab in the thirty-eighth year of Asa (1 Kings 16:29). Thus Omri reigned from sometime during the twenty-seventh

year of Asa (ending 15 Tishri 879) until the thirty-eighth year of Asa
(ending 15 Tishri 868). His rule, therefore, extended over twelve of
Asa's years although this would have constituted only eleven regnal
year periods in the north (from 15 Marheshvan 879 until after 15
Marheshvan 869). The calculation giving him twelve years seems to
have been made in terms of the years of Asa rather than in terms of
actual Israelite regnal years. This was probably due to two factors.
First, Omri was confronted with civil war in the north which began in
Asa's twenty-seventh year and lasted for parts of five Judean years
(from before 15 Tishri 879 until after 15 Tishri 876). The accession
formula in 1 Kings 16:23 implies that Omri's twelve-year reign began
in the thirty-first year of Asa, but this is contradicted by 16:29. Thus
there appears to have been some confusion in the sources used by
the editors of Kings resulting from the uncertainty about the actual
point at which Omri began to reign. Second, the sources noted that
he ruled for six years in Tirzah before founding the new royal city of
Samaria (1 Kings 16:23b-24). This was a calculation based on Judean
reckoning (from before 15 Tishri 879 until after 15 Tishri 875).
Samaria was thus founded sometime after 15 Marheshvan 875 but
before 15 Marheshvan 874. Omri then reigned for six regnal years in
Samaria. His twelve years of rule were computed by calculating the
six years' rule in Tirzah plus six regnal years in Samaria.

  Ahab succeeded to the throne in Samaria in the thirty-eighth
year of Asa (869-868; 1 Kings 16:29a). He is said to have ruled
twenty-two years (1 Kings 16:29b). Because of the difficulties
involved in synchronizing a reign of twenty-two years, we have
assumed that Ahab reigned for fifteen years. One firm fact is
known: he was reigning in Samaria at the time of the battle of Qarqar in the summer of 853. His fifteenth year began, according to our
reckoning, with 15 Marheshvan 854 and would not have ended until
15 Marheshvan 853. As we shall see below, various chronological
and literary problems cloud the reign of Jehoshaphat, Ahab's contemporary, and these may have influenced the editorial assignment
of years to Ahab. On the other hand, Ahab's death in 853 occurred
twenty-two years after the founding of Samaria in 875 and twenty-
two Judean regnal years after the founding of Samaria if he died
after 15 Tishri 853. Calculation of his death date from the founding
of the new Israelite capital thus was probably the source of the
twenty-two year reference. (As we have noted, Omri's reign too was
partially computed in terms of the founding of Samaria; see 1 Kings
16:23-24.)

The reign of Ahab provides the first occasion when an Israelite king can be associated with some event known from extra-biblical sources. He is mentioned in an inscription of Shalmaneser III (858-824). Shalmaneser reports on his Black Obelisk that during his first regnal year he marched westward, eventually reaching the Mediterranean Sea (*ARAB* I § 558). In his Monolith Inscription, he notes that he was opposed at that time by several rulers in northern Syria (*ARAB* I § 600; *ANET* 277). In his sixth year (853-852), Shalmaneser departed Nineveh in early spring (14 Iyyar) and, after some fighting east of the Euphrates (*ARAB* I § 610), crossed the river and at Qarqar fought a coalition headed by Irhuleni of Hamath. The coalition army consisted of troops from a number of states extending from western Anatolia to Egypt. Listed as part of the coalition's force were 2,000 chariots and 10,000 soldiers of Ahab (*ARAB* I § 611; *ANET* 278-79). The battle of Qarqar was fought in the summer of 853, during Ahab's fifteenth year. Notably absent from the list of participants at the battle among Syro-Palestinian states are Moab, Edom, and Judah, although even the Arabs are represented. This is best explained by assuming that Moab, Edom, and Judah were dominated at the time by Israel--in fact, were vassal states--and their troops were numbered among Israel's force.

In his tenth, eleventh, and fourteenth years, Shalmaneser again fought the western coalition (*ANET* 279-80; *ARAB* I §§ 558-59, 568, 571, 658-59). The coalition thus remained intact from at least 853 until 845. Although Shalmaneser only names the members of this coalition once, it is safe to assume that the Israelite king remained a functioning member until its dissolution in 845.

Jehoshaphat's reign presents numerous difficulties for historians, in terms of both chronology and depiction. Several factors contribute to the difficulties. His name and that of Ahab appear to have been introduced secondarily into the prophetic stories of 1 Kings 22:1-40. In addition, the originally unnamed Israelite king of the stories in 1 Kings 20-21 was later identified as Ahab. Practically all the Elisha traditions in 2 Kings 1:2-2:25; 3:9b-25; and 4:1-8:15 concern events during the time of the Jehu dynasty. These narratives have been secondarily related to the period before the rise of Jehu to power, further complicating the presentation of the history. Finally, Asa appears to have abdicated the throne in his twenty-ninth year (sometime after 15 Tishri 878) although he lived an additional twelve years (until after 15 Tishri 866). First Kings 15:23b notes that in "his old age Asa was diseased in the feet," which would seem to be the reason for his abdication. The editors, however, assumed that Jehoshaphat's twenty-five year reign (1 Kings 22:42) occurred after Asa's forty-first year and have posited synchronisms on this basis. Thus the synchronisms between the beginning of Jehoshaphat's reign and the fourth year of Ahab in 1 Kings 22:41, the association of the beginning of Ahaziah's reign with Jehoshaphat's seventeenth year in 1 Kings 22:51a, and the association of the beginning of Jehoram's rule with Jehoshaphat's eighteenth year in 2 Kings 3:1 are based on placing the twenty-five years of Jehoshaphat's reign after Asa's forty-one years and therefore must be discounted.

According to our reconstruction, Jehoshaphat's twenty-five year reign ended before 15 Tishri 852. It thus overlapped part of the brief reign of Ahaziah (1 Kings 22:51b; see v. 49). Ahaziah's reign was short-lived because of injuries received in a fall (2 Kings 1:2). His injury probably occurred very early in his reign if not in his accession year. If Jehoram and Jehoshaphat along with the vassal ruler in Edom (1 Kings 22:47; 2 Kings 3:12b, 26) carried out an unsuccessful joint campaign to retake Moab (2 Kings 3:4-9a, 26-27), which had revolted at the time of Ahab's death (2 Kings 1:1), this would have occurred while Jehoram was helping run affairs in Samaria on behalf of his brother-in-law, the injured Ahaziah.

5. JEHORAM AND AHAZIAH

JUDAH
JEHORAM (852-841)

0. ....- Tishri 852
1. Tishri 852 - Tishri 851
2. Tishri 851 - Tishri 850
3. Tishri 850 - Tishri 849
4. Tishri 849 - Tishri 848
5. Tishri 848 - Tishri 847
6. Tishri 847 - Tishri 846
7. Tishri 846 - Tishri 845
8. Tishri 845 - ....

AHAZIAH (840)

0. ....- Tishri 840
1. Tishri 840 - ....

ISRAEL
JEHORAM (851-840)

0. ....- Marheshvan 851
1. Marheshvan 851 - Marheshvan 850
2. Marheshvan 850 - Marheshvan 849
3. Marheshvan 849 - Marheshvan 848
4. Marheshvan 848 - Marheshvan 847
5. Marheshvan 847 - Marheshvan 846
6. Marheshvan 846 - Marheshvan 845
7. Marheshvan 845 - Marheshvan 844
8. Marheshvan 844 - Marheshvan 843
9. Marheshvan 843 - Marheshvan 842
10. Marheshvan 842 - Marheshvan 841
11. Marheshvan 841 - Marheshvan 840
12. Marheshvan 840 - ....

ASSYRIA
SHALMANESER III (858-824)

8. Nisan 851 - Nisan 850
9. Nisan 850 - Nisan 849
10. Nisan 849 - Nisan 848
11. Nisan 848 - Nisan 847
12. Nisan 847 - Nisan 846
13. Nisan 846 - Nisan 845
14. Nisan 845 - Nisan 844
15. Nisan 844 - Nisan 843
16. Nisan 843 - Nisan 842
17. Nisan 842 - Nisan 841
18. Nisan 841 - Nisan 840
19. Nisan 840 - Nisan 839

5. Jehoram and Ahaziah

P. K. **McCarter**, "'Yaw, Son of 'Omri': A Philological Note on Israelite Chronology," *BASOR* 216(1974)5-7; J. **Strange**, "Joram, King of Israel and Judah," *VT* 25(1975)191-201; E. R. **Thiele**, "An Additional Chronological Note on 'Yaw, Son of 'Omri,'" *BASOR* 222(1976)19-23; M. **Weippert**, "Jau(a) Mar Ḫumrî--Joram oder Jehu von Israel?," *VT* 28(1978)113-18.

Our reconstruction of the chronology of this period is based on two hypotheses. First, Jehoram of Israel and Jehoram of Judah were the same person, namely the son of Jehoshaphat; for a period of just over a decade a Davidic monarch ruled over both houses of Israel for the first time since the death of Solomon. Second, the difference in years between Jehoram's eight-year reign in Jerusalem (2 Kings 8:17) and his twelve-year reign in Samaria (2 Kings 3:1b) can be explained on the basis of the international situation.

The final editors of the Kings material assumed that Jehoram of Israel was a son of Ahab. Three texts clearly make this connection (2 Kings 8:16, 25; 9:29). The first of these texts, however, is garbled. The passage literally reads: "In the fifth year of Joram son of Ahab king of Israel and Jehoshaphat king of Judah, Jehoram son of Jehoshaphat began to rule as king of Judah." The other two texts are clear in their present form.

A fourth text relevant to the issue is 2 Kings 1:17, which reads: "And thus he [Ahaziah] died according to the word of the Lord which Elijah had spoken and Jehoram began to rule in his place in the second year of Jehoram son of Jehoshaphat king of Judah because he [Ahaziah] had no son." Some of the ancient versions add "his brother" after the first "Jehoram."

We would propose that the identification of Jehoram as a son of Ahab or a brother of Ahaziah represents secondary editorial activity. The statements about Ahaziah in 2 Kings 1:2-18 before the introduction of the Elijah material (vv. 2b-17*) probably read:

> And Ahaziah fell through the lattice of his upper chamber in Samaria and lay sick. When he died Jehoram began to rule in his stead in the second year of Jehoram son of Jehoshaphat king of Judah because he (Ahaziah) had no son. And the rest

of the deeds of Ahaziah which he did, are not they written in
the book of the days of the kings of Israel? (2:1a, 17*-18).

At the later editorial stage, when confronted with references to an
unspecified Jehoram ruling in Samaria who was declared not to be a
son of Ahaziah, editors assumed him to be a son of Ahab.

In addition, the synchronisms in 1 Kings 22:41, 51; 2 Kings 3:1;
and 8:16, are secondary editorial synchronisms. Apparently the
editors of Kings inherited sources containing all of the synchronisms
up to the point at which the Elijah-Elisha stories were incorporated
(1 Kings 17). These synchronisms were left intact. The editors then
worked to integrate the Elijah-Elisha traditions and similar
prophetic narratives placing all of them (except 2 Kings 9; 13:14-21)
into what was assumed to be an Omride context. Chronologically,
the editors were confronted with the need to devise synchronisms
from the thirty-eighth year of Asa (= first year of Ahab; 1 Kings
16:29) until Jehoram and Ahaziah (son of Jehoram) were killed by
Jehu. Thus they had to correlate 3 remaining years for Asa, plus 25
for Jehoshaphat, plus 8 for Jehoram, plus 1 year for Ahaziah (37 in
all) with Ahab's 22 years, plus 2 years for Ahaziah, plus 12 years for
Jehoram of Israel (36 in all). (It could have been at this stage that
Ahab's reign was extended from 15 to 22 years.) The synchronisms
in 1 Kings 22:41, 51; 2 Kings 3:1; and 8:16 were made on this basis.

Second Kings 1:17 preserves the older and correct synchronism.
Jehoshaphat died after 15 Tishri 853 and was succeeded on the
throne in Jerusalem by his son Jehoram, who was already assisting in
the rule of the north for the injured Ahaziah. If Jehoshaphat and
Jehoram carried out a joint but unsuccessful Israelite and Judean
campaign to reconquer Moab (2 Kings 3:4-9a; 26-27), it would have
probably occurred in the spring or summer of 852, shortly after the
battle of Qarqar in the summer of 853, at a time when the troops
were already mustered, and before the death of Jehoshaphat and the
revolt of Edom (2 Kings 8:20). With the death of Jehoshaphat,
Jehoram succeeded to the Judean throne, before 15 Tishri 852.

With the death of Ahaziah of Israel, after 15 Tishri 851 (the
beginning of Jehoram's second year in Judah [2 Kings 1:17]),
Jehoram took over the throne in Samaria as well. 2 Chron. 21:4 may
preserve some memory of Jehoram's solidification of his hold on
both thrones: when he occupied the throne in Samaria, Jehoram
exterminated any immediate threats to his reign in both the south
and the north.

Jehoram took over a rapidly deteriorating situation. The old Israel/Judah/Moab/Edom coalition ruled over by the Omrides was moving toward total disintegration. Moab under King Mesha asserted its independence with the death of Ahab and consolidated its holdings (2 Kings 1:1; *ANET* 320-21), a move aided by the injury to Ahaziah which left Israel without effective Omride leadership. The Edomites revolted shortly after the death of Jehoshaphat, and Jehoram was unable to bring them back under Judean control (2 Kings 8:20-22a). Even a major Judean city, Libnah, located just east of Philistine territory in the southwest of Judah, proclaimed its independence from Jerusalem (2 Kings 8:22b).

Jehoram is attributed twelve years of rule in Samaria (2 Kings 3:1), which we date from before 15 Marheshvan 851 until after 15 Marheshvan 840. He is assigned only eight years in Jerusalem (2 Kings 8:17) and was succeeded in Jerusalem by his son Ahaziah in his eleventh or twelfth year (2 Kings 8:25; 9:29). What appears to be a rather odd set of facts is understandable in light of the international circumstances at the time.

In his sixth year, in the summer of 853, Shalmaneser III fought the anti-Assyrian western coalition at the battle of Qarqar. The combined Israelite/Judean/Moabite/Edomite force was led by King Ahab. In his eleventh year (or tenth, according to the fragmentary annals from Calah; *ARAB* I §§ 651-52), Shalmaneser again fought this coalition under the leadership of Hadadezer of Damascus and Irhuleni of Hamath (*ARAB* I §§ 568, 654; *ANET* 280). This would have been in 848-847 (or 849-848). The Israelite/Judean force (Moab and Edom had revolted from Israelite/Judean control; 2 Kings 1:1; 8:20) would have been led by Jehoram. In his fourteenth year (845-844), Shalmaneser marched west again and fought this coalition for the fourth time (*ARAB* I §§ 571, 659, 691; *ANET* 280-81). On a basalt statue, Shalmaneser describes this battle in detail:

> At that time I defeated Hadad-ezer of Syria together with 12 princes, his allies, 29,000 warriors, his fighters I brought low. .... The rest of his armies I pushed into the Orontes River. To save their lives they dispersed. Hadad-ezer died. Hazael, the son of a nobody seized the throne, mustered his large army and came out against me, offering battle and fight. I fought with and defeated him, capturing the chariots of his camp. To save his life he fled. I advanced as far as Damascus

his royal city and cut down his orchards (see *ARAB* § 681;
ANET 280).

Thus in late 845 or early 844, two significant events occurred. First,
Shalmaneser decisively defeated the western coalition with Hadadezer dying in or at the time of the battle. Second, Hazael usurped
the throne in Damascus and was left to fight Assyria alone;
presumably, the other states in the coalition abandoned the field.
Hazael thus became king of Damascus probably sometime in 844,
perhaps after Nisan 844.

The year 845-844 was the last regnal year attributed to Jehoram
in Jerusalem. The reason for this was the following: Hazael made
no immediate effort to reestablish the coalition and, in fact, began
hostile action against Israel. With the Syrians now Israel's enemies,
Jehoram was preoccupied in the north and did not return to
Jerusalem for the celebration of the fall festival after 15 Tishri 845.
Presumably his son Ahaziah served for a time as administrator in the
south but without being installed as king. The combined
Israelite/Judean forces under Jehoram and Ahaziah were hard
pressed to defend their Transjordanian territory against Hazael (2
Kings 8:28a). Jehoram was wounded in battle at Ramoth-gilead,
probably early in his eleventh year as king in Samaria (15 Marheshvan 841 to 15 Marheshvan 840; 2 Kings 8:28b; 9:14b-15a). With the
wounding of Jehoram, Ahaziah assumed the throne in Judah (2
Kings 9:29). At the next fall festival (15 Tishri 840), Ahaziah was
anointed and installed as king of Judah (2 Kings 8:25). Ahaziah
would thus have become king in Jerusalem in the twelfth year following Jehoram's coronation over Judah (see 2 Kings 8:25) and his
eleventh year in Samaria (see 2 Kings 9:29). Apparently references
to the date of Ahaziah's assumption of the throne were preserved in
both Israelite (2 Kings 9:29) and Judean (2 Kings 8:25) records.
(Note that the reference to the twelfth year in 2 Kings 8:25 occurs in
the context of Judean narratives and that the reference to the
eleventh year in 2 Kings 9:29 appears in the context of Israelite narratives.) Shortly after the installation, Ahaziah went north, perhaps
to run the government for his ailing father who was then at the
winter palace in Jezreel recuperating from his wounds (2 Kings
8:29). Both were exterminated in an Israelite revolt led by Jehu.

6. FROM JEHU TO JEROBOAM II

JUDAH

ATHALIAH (839-833)

0. .... - Tishri 839
1. Tishri 839 - Tishri 838
2. Tishri 838 - Tishri 837
3. Tishri 837 - Tishri 836
4. Tishri 836 - Tishri 835
5. Tishri 835 - Tishri 834
6. Tishri 834 - Tishri 833
7. Tishri 833 - ....

JEHOASH (832-803[791])

0. .... - Tishri 832
1. Tishri 832 - Tishri 831
2. Tishri 831 - Tishri 830
3. Tishri 830 - Tishri 829
4. Tishri 829 - Tishri 828
5. Tishri 828 - Tishri 827
6. Tishri 827 - Tishri 826
7. Tishri 826 - Tishri 825
8. Tishri 825 - Tishri 824
9. Tishri 824 - Tishri 823

ISRAEL

JEHU (839-822)

0. .... - Marheshvan 839
1. Marheshvan 839 - Marheshvan 838
2. Marheshvan 838 - Marheshvan 837
3. Marheshvan 837 - Marheshvan 836
4. Marheshvan 836 - Marheshvan 835
5. Marheshvan 835 - Marheshvan 834
6. Marheshvan 834 - Marheshvan 833
7. Marheshvan 833 - Marheshvan 832
8. Marheshvan 832 - Marheshvan 831
9. Marheshvan 831 - Marheshvan 830
10. Marheshvan 830 - Marheshvan 829
11. Marheshvan 829 - Marheshvan 828
12. Marheshvan 828 - Marheshvan 827
13. Marheshvan 827 - Marheshvan 826
14. Marheshvan 826 - Marheshvan 825
15. Marheshvan 825 - Marheshvan 824
16. Marheshvan 824 - Marheshvan 823

ASSYRIA

SHALMANESER III (858-824)

20. Nisan 839 - Nisan 838
21. Nisan 838 - Nisan 837
22. Nisan 837 - Nisan 836
23. Nisan 836 - Nisan 835
24. Nisan 835 - Nisan 834
25. Nisan 834 - Nisan 833
26. Nisan 833 - Nisan 832
27. Nisan 832 - Nisan 831
28. Nisan 831 - Nisan 830
29. Nisan 830 - Nisan 829
30. Nisan 829 - Nisan 828
31. Nisan 828 - Nisan 827
32. Nisan 827 - Nisan 826
33. Nisan 826 - Nisan 825
34. Nisan 825 - Nisan 824
35. Nisan 824 - ....

SHAMSHI-ADAD V (823-811)

0. .... - Nisan 823
1. Nisan 823 - Nisan 822
2. Nisan 822 - Nisan 821
3. Nisan 821 - Nisan 820
4. Nisan 820 - Nisan 819
5. Nisan 819 - Nisan 818
6. Nisan 818 - Nisan 817
7. Nisan 817 - Nisan 816
8. Nisan 816 - Nisan 815
9. Nisan 815 - Nisan 814
10. Nisan 814 - Nisan 813
11. Nisan 813 - Nisan 812
12. Nisan 812 - Nisan 811
13. Nisan 811 - ....

ADAD-NIRARI III (810-783)

0. .... - Nisan 810
1. Nisan 810 - Nisan 809
2. Nisan 809 - Nisan 808
3. Nisan 808 - Nisan 807
4. Nisan 807 - Nisan 806
5. Nisan 806 - Nisan 805
6. Nisan 805 - Nisan 804

---

17. Marheshvan 823 - Marheshvan 822
18. Marheshvan 822 - ....

JEHOAHAZ (821-805)

0. .... - Marheshvan 821
1. Marheshvan 821 - Marheshvan 820
2. Marheshvan 820 - Marheshvan 819
3. Marheshvan 819 - Marheshvan 818
4. Marheshvan 818 - Marheshvan 817
5. Marheshvan 817 - Marheshvan 816
6. Marheshvan 816 - Marheshvan 815
7. Marheshvan 815 - Marheshvan 814
8. Marheshvan 814 - Marheshvan 813
9. Marheshvan 813 - Marheshvan 812
10. Marheshvan 812 - Marheshvan 811
11. Marheshvan 811 - Marheshvan 810
12. Marheshvan 810 - Marheshvan 809
13. Marheshvan 809 - Marheshvan 808
14. Marheshvan 808 - Marheshvan 807
15. Marheshvan 807 - Marheshvan 806
16. Marheshvan 806 - Marheshvan 805
17. Marheshvan 805 - ....

---

10. Tishri 823 - Tishri 822
11. Tishri 822 - Tishri 821
12. Tishri 821 - Tishri 820
13. Tishri 820 - Tishri 819
14. Tishri 819 - Tishri 818
15. Tishri 818 - Tishri 817
16. Tishri 817 - Tishri 816
17. Tishri 816 - Tishri 815
18. Tishri 815 - Tishri 814
19. Tishri 814 - Tishri 813
20. Tishri 813 - Tishri 812
21. Tishri 812 - Tishri 811
22. Tishri 811 - Tishri 810
23. Tishri 810 - Tishri 809
24. Tishri 809 - Tishri 808
25. Tishri 808 - Tishri 807
26. Tishri 807 - Tishri 806
27. Tishri 806 - Tishri 805
28. Tishri 805 - Tishri 804

JEHOASH (804-789)

0. .... - Marheshvan 804
1. Marheshvan 804 - Marheshvan 803
2. Marheshvan 803 - Marheshvan 802

7. Nisan 804 - Nisan 803
8. Nisan 803 - Nisan 802

3. Marheshvan 802 - Marheshvan 801
4. Marheshvan 801 - Marheshvan 800
5. Marheshvan 800 - Marheshvan 799
6. Marheshvan 799 - Marheshvan 798
7. Marheshvan 798 - Marheshvan 797
8. Marheshvan 797 - Marheshvan 796
9. Marheshvan 796 - Marheshvan 795
10. Marheshvan 795 - Marheshvan 794
11. Marheshvan 794 - Marheshvan 793
12. Marheshvan 793 - Marheshvan 792
13. Marheshvan 792 - Marheshvan 791
14. Marheshvan 791 - Marheshvan 790
15. Marheshvan 790 - Marheshvan 789
16. Marheshvan 789 - ....

9. Nisan 802 - Nisan 801
10. Nisan 801 - Nisan 800
11. Nisan 800 - Nisan 799
12. Nisan 799 - Nisan 798
13. Nisan 798 - Nisan 797
14. Nisan 797 - Nisan 796
15. Nisan 796 - Nisan 795
16. Nisan 795 - Nisan 794
17. Nisan 794 - Nisan 793
18. Nisan 793 - Nisan 792
19. Nisan 792 - Nisan 791
20. Nisan 791 - Nisan 790
21. Nisan 790 - Nisan 789
22. Nisan 789 - Nisan 788

29. Tishri 804 - Tishri 803
30. Tishri 803 - ....

AMAZIAH (802-786[774])
0. .... - Tishri 802

(Jehoash)

1. Tishri 802 - Tishri 801 (31)
2. Tishri 801 - Tishri 800 (32)
3. Tishri 800 - Tishri 799 (33)
4. Tishri 799 - Tishri 798 (34)
5. Tishri 798 - Tishri 797 (35)
6. Tishri 797 - Tishri 796 (36)
7. Tishri 796 - Tishri 795 (37)
8. Tishri 795 - Tishri 794 (38)
9. Tishri 794 - Tishri 793 (39)
10. Tishri 793 - Tishri 792 (40)
11. Tishri 792 - Tishri 791
12. Tishri 791 - Tishri 790
13. Tishri 790 - Tishri 789
14. Tishri 789 - Tishri 788

6. From Jehu to Jeroboam II

M. C. **Astour**, "841 B.C.: The First Assyrian Invasion of Israel," *JAOS* 91(1971)383-89; J. A. **Dearman** and J. M. **Miller**, "The Melqart Stele and the Ben Hadads of Damascus: Two Studies," *PEQ* 115(1983)95-101; M. **Elat**, "The Campaigns of Shalmaneser III Against Aram and Israel," *IEJ* 25(1975)25-35; M. **Haran**, "The Rise and Decline of the Empire of Jeroboam ben Joash," *VT* 17(1967)266-97; A. **Jepsen**, "Israel und Damaskus," *AfO* 14(1941-44)153-72; A. R. **Millard** and H. **Tadmor**, "Adad-nirari III in Syria: Another Stele Fragment and the Dates of His Campaigns," *Iraq* 35(1973)57-64; J. M. **Miller**, "The Fall of the House of Ahab," *VT* 17(1967) 307-24; **Miller**, "The Rest of the Acts of Jehoahaz (I Kings 20; 22:1-38)," *ZAW* 80(1968)337-42; **Miller**, "The Moabite Stone as a Memorial Stela," *PEQ* 106(1974)9-18; S. **Page**, "A Stela of Adad-nirari and Nergal-eresh from Tell al Rimah," *Iraq* 30(1968)139-53; W. T. **Pitard**, *Ancient Damascus: A Historical Study of the Syrian City-State from Earliest Times Until Its Fall to the Assyrians in 732 B.C.E.* (Winona Lake, IN: Eisenbrauns, 1987); W. H. **Shea**, "Adad-nirari III and Jehoash of Israel," *JCS* 30(1978)101-13; C. C. **Smith**, "Jehu and the Black Obelisk of Shalmaneser III," *Scripture in History and Theology: Essays in Honor of J. Coert Rylaarsdam* (ed. A. A. Merrill and T. W. Overholt; Pittsburgh: Pickwick Press, 1977)71-105; H. **Tadmor**, "The Historical Inscriptions of Adad-nirari III," *Iraq* 35(1973)141-50.

The account of Jehu's seizure of the throne in Samaria is found in 2 Kings 9:1-10:28. Three facts about this material should be noted in assessing its value for chronological and historical reconstruction.

First, it was shaped as political propaganda on behalf of the Jehu dynasty probably late in the reign of Jeroboam II. When the state was threatened militarily and the dynasty came under the sharp criticism of the prophets Hosea (1:4-5) and Amos (7:9-11), the story of Jehu's rise was used to portray the dynasty as the defender of the nation and its religion. In the material, the house of Ahab is therefore depicted as the primary source of apostasy for the nation. Jehu is described as the great defender of Yahwism, the savior of the people from the house of Ahab, and the exterminator of Baalism. Jehu's rise is traced back to the prophetic hero Elijah (see Hos.

12:13b). The pro-dynastic version of the story no doubt spoke of Elijah as the prophet who sent his servant (Elisha) to anoint Jehu. When the majority of the Elisha materials became associated with the "Omride" period, thus preceding chapter 9, Elisha replaced Elijah in this and perhaps other stories (see 1 Kings 19:15-18; 2 Kings 8:7-15).

Second, the story has greatly telecoped events. In the propaganda version, Jehu's anointing, his killing of Jehoram (understood as an Omride!) and Ahaziah, his takeover of Samaria, and the slaughter of Baal worshipers are depicted as occurring within a very short time and with the support of the general population. The events undoubtedly took a much longer time and probably involved military actions.

Third, no allusion is made to Jehu's pro-Assyrian stance or to the fact that he was probably encouraged by Shalmaneser III to seize the throne and rule.

The chronology of Jehu's takeover of the Israelite throne must be viewed in light of international political developments. In his eighteenth year (841-840), Shalmaneser again campaigned to the west. He describes the following events during the course of that campaign.

> I crossed the Euphrates for the sixteenth time. Hazael of Damascus put his trust in his large army and called up his troops in great number, making Mount Senir, a mountain peak facing the Lebanons, his stronghold. I fought with him and defeated him, killing 16,000 of his warriors with the sword. I took away from him 1,121 chariots, 470 of his horses, as well as his camp. To save his life, he took flight. I followed after him. I shut him up in Damascus his royal city. His orchards I cut down. I advanced as far as Mount Hauran. Countless cities I destroyed, I devastated, I burned with fire. Their spoil, beyond counting I carried away. I marched to Mount Ba'li-rasi, at the side of the sea and erected there my royal image. At that time, I received the tribute of the people of Tyre, Sidon, and of Jehu, ruler of Omri-land (see *ARAB* I § 672; *ANET* 280).

Thus in 841-840, Shalmaneser defeated Hazael, marched through and burned much of the northern Transjordan, made his way to

Ba'li-rasi (probably the area of the Dog River near modern Beirut where monarchs through history set up their inscriptions) and received tribute gifts. Among those presenting gifts was Jehu (see *ARAB* I § 590; *ANET* 281).

One can imagine the following course of events in Jehu's rise. The Israelite forces defending Transjordan against Syria were confronted with the option of fighting or not fighting Assyria, now battling Syria. In spite of a previous history of cooperation with Syria against Assyria, Jehu chose to submit to Assyria and offer tribute. In exchange, he was recognized by Shalmaneser as the new ruler of Omri-land. Shalmaneser, after all, was merely returning the Israelite throne to an Israelite, after the Davidic "interregnum." With King Jehoram ill and miles from the battlefield, the Israelite army under Jehu was free to choose its own course of action as it had some four decades earlier when it declared Omri king, and thus went along with the new conditions. Jehu's submission to Assyria must have been made sometime in late 841 or early 840. It established a pro-Assyrian stance that characterized Israelite politics for over a hundred years, until the time of Pekah.

Jehu was declared king but had yet to win control of his kingdom. Evidently this was no easy matter; even a favorable narrative speaks of enormous bloodshed (2 Kings 10:11). In the struggle, Jehoram, Ahaziah, and most of the two royal families, Omride and Davidic, were exterminated. Samaria finally came under Jehu's control, perhaps surrendering to avoid a siege. The slaughter of the royal families and the takeover of Samaria probably occurred after 15 Marheshvan 840 since 840-839 was attributed to Jehoram. Jehu's first regnal year thus would have been 839-838.

In the south, Athaliah, the Omride wife of the deceased Jehoram, assumed control of the government. In spite of the negative portrayal of her rule in 2 Kings 11:1-16, she must have enjoyed some popular support during her seven-year tenure. Two factors were in her favor. First, whether or not Jehu, in assassinating both Jehoram and Ahaziah, had intended to rule a combined Israel and Judah, Athaliah at least preserved the integrity of the Judean throne. Secondly, as a princess with Tyrian royal connections, Athaliah could appeal to the history of close Jerusalemite-Tyre connections. The importance of Tyre in Judean history was enormous (see 2 Sam. 5:11; 1 Kings 5:1-12; 9:10-14, 26-28; 10:11-12, 22; Ps. 45:12). Third Kings 5:1 in the Greek has preserved a tradition, probably delib-

erately altered in the Hebrew, which could indicate that David and
Solomon had functioned as vassals to Hiram: "And Hiram king of
Tyre sent his officials to anoint Solomon in place of David. . . ."

The assigned length of Jehu's reign and the synchronisms for
the early kings of the Jehu dynasty (Jehoahaz and Jehoash) except
for 2 Kings 12:1; 14:1 (where Judean kings are synchronized with
their Israelite counterparts, rather than vice versa) are somewhat
peculiar in that they show variations from the expected specifics of
any Judean/Israelite synchronization. Jehoahaz should have been
noted as becoming king of Israel in Jehoash's twenty-first or twenty-
second year (with seven of Jehu's years paralleling the seven years
for Athaliah), rather than his twenty-third year (2 Kings 13:1).
Jehoash of Israel should have become king in Jehoash of Judah's
thirty-eighth or thirty-ninth year (the combined reigns of Jehu and
Jehoahaz equalling forty-five years minus the seven years of
Athaliah), rather than his thirty-seventh year (2 Kings 13:10). It may
be that these synchronisms are late editorial calculations and thus
not exactly accurate.

We propose, however, the following origin for the figures in 2
Kings 10:36; 13:1, 10. The twenty-eight years assigned Jehu are not
given as part of any accession year formula but are a summary statement at the end of the description of his reign. The figure of twenty-
eight years originally represented not the number of years of his
reign but the number of full regnal years between his last regnal year
(823-822) and the first full regnal year of his predecessor Jehoram
(851-850), when the Israelite state in the north was temporarily
usurped by a Davidic monarch.

The twenty-third year and the thirty-seventh year referred to as
the beginning of the reigns of Jehoahaz and Jehoash cannot be correlated with any Judean monarch. The only correlation which even
comes close to fitting the synchronisms is with the reign of Hazael of
Syria. Throughout the last third of the ninth century Israel and other
states were vassals to Syria under Hazael and Ben-hadad (2 Kings
13:3), a situation reflected in the Elisha narratives. Jehu had quickly
lost all of Transjordan to Hazael (2 Kings 10:32-33), and during most
of his reign and that of Jehoahaz, Israel, and perhaps Judah, were
Syrian vassals. Even Gath and Jerusalem were threatened with siege
by Hazael (2 Kings 12:17). Israel, except for the city-state of
Samaria, appears to have been administered during this period by
Syria. Governors were placed over Israelite districts (1 Kings 20:14-

15). (The Israelite tribal lists in the book of Joshua may derive from this period of Syrian dominance and reflect Syrian administrative districts. The Samaria ostraca which give the year [from nine to seventeen] but not the name of a reigning monarch belong to this period and could be dated on the basis of the reign of Hazael, possibly representing the collection of tribute taxes for Syria. According to our calculation of the beginning of Hazael's first regnal year in Nisan 843, the ninth, tenth, fifteenth, and seventeenth years of Hazael, represented on the Samaria ostraca, would have been 835-834, 834-833, 829-828, and 827-826.)

Jehoahaz assumed the throne in Samaria in 822-821, after Nisan 821, in the twenty-third year of Hazael. The thirty-seventh year is probably a similar synchronism. Although the figure appears low since the thirty-seventh year of Hazael (on a Nisan to Nisan calendar) would most likely have been 807-806, it may have been that Jehoash was running the government or the military by that time because of an injury to Jehoahaz, received in battle against Syria. Jehoash apparently assumed the throne very early in 805-804.

At the tender age of seven, Jehoash of Judah ascended the throne in the seventh year of Jehu's reign (2 Kings 11:21-12:1), at the fall festival in 832. He was subsequently forced to abdicate, according to our calculations, before Tishri 802, having been injured in an assassination attempt. The verb describing the action of the conspirators in 2 Kings 12:20-21 does not mean "kill," as it is rendered in most modern translations, but "attack" or "wound." The same verb is used to describe what the Syrians did to Jehoram in battle at Ramoth-gilead (2 Kings 8:28), after which Jehoram survived (see 2 Kings 15:25, 30 and compare 14:19). Second Kings 12:20-21 should be translated:

> His servants plotted and formed a conspiracy and wounded (or attacked) Jehoash at Beth-millo on the way down to Silla. His servants who wounded him were Jozabad son of Shimeath and Jozabad son of Shomer. When he died they (the people) buried him with his fathers in the city of David, and Amaziah his son reigned in his place.

Even though the material has been edited here, as generally throughout Kings, so as to finish completely the description of a king's life and death before discussing the next ruler, the conspiracy

did not result in Jehoash's death. He was wounded and had to abdicate the throne in his thirtieth year (after 15 Tishri 803) but continued to live for another ten years (until after Tishri 793).

The reason for the conspiracy against Jehoash is not given.
Only two events are explicitly reported for his reign: how he raised
funds to repair the temple (2 Kings 12:4-16) and how he emptied the
temple and royal treasuries to buy off Hazael who was threatening to
lay Jerusalem under siege (2 Kings 12:17-18). In both narratives,
Jehoash is depicted as a weak, unaggressive monarch. In the period
just prior to the attempted assassination, Jehoash was a subservient
partner in Israel's wars against Syria (see below). His would-be
assassins probably sought to remove him from office so he could be
replaced by a stronger, nationalistic leader.

One allusion to international affairs during the reign of
Jehoahaz, a contemporary of Jehoash of Judah, is made in 2 Kings
13:5. This passage reports that during (apparently near the end of)
Jehoahaz's reign "God gave Israel a savior so that they were
delivered from the hand of Syria and the Israelites dwelt in their
tents as formerly"; that is, they were freed from complete vassalage
to Syria and were able, at least temporarily, to return to running
their own affairs. This situation alludes to the revival of Assyrian
pressure in the west. Shalmaneser III had made his last western
campaign in his twenty-first year (838-837) and it was not until
Adad-nirari III (810-783) that Assyrian pressure was again felt in the
west, where Syria was now the head of a great anti-Assyrian alliance
forged by Hazael. In the opening sections of his Rimah stela, Adad-
nirari describes, with typical monarchical braggadocio, a major
western campaign:

> I mobilized chariots, troops and camps, and ordered a
> campaign to Hatti land. In a single year I made the land of
> Amurru and the Hatti land in its entirety kneel at my feet; I
> imposed tribute and regular tax for future days upon them.
>
> I marched to the great sea where the sun sets [the
> Mediterranean], and erected an image of my royal self in the
> city of Arvad which is in the middle of the sea. I went up the
> Lebanon mountains and cut down timbers: one hundred
> mature cedars, material needed for my palace and temples
> (*Iraq* 35 [1973]) 143; see also *ANET* 281-82; *ARAB* I §§ 734-
> 35, 739-40).

In all probability, it was the Assyrian *turtanu* Shamshi-ilu who carried out the western campaigns and was thus Jehoahaz's actual savior rather than Adad-nirari himself. Adad-nirari III also mentions the complete humiliation of Damascus (see the texts listed at the end of the above quotation and below). The revival of Assyrian influence gave Israel the opportunity to begin asserting its independence after over three decades of vassal servitude to Syria. This illustrates political dynamics characteristic of the late ninth and eighth centuries: a strong Assyria actively involved in western politics resulted in a strong Israel and a weak Syria; a weak Assyria resulted in a strong Syria and a weak Israel. (The events behind the narratives of 1 Kings 20 and 22:1-38 originally concerned Jehoahaz's initial reassertion, assisted by the Judean Jehoash, of Israelite independence from Syria.)

According to our chronology, Jehoahaz died after 15 Marheshvan 805, perhaps a casualty of injuries received in the Israelite/Judean wars with Syria. (See 1 Kings 22:29-37, a highly reworked and dramatized narrative in which the events are related to kings Ahab and Jehoshaphat rather than Jehoahaz of Israel and Jehoash of Judah.) After having suffered a final, humiliating defeat, Jehoahaz was succeeded by Jehoash of Israel (before 15 Marheshvan 804), who inherited the throne with Israel still a Syrian vassal (1 Kings 13:7), but quickly renewed the wars to recover Israelite territory from Syria. Adad-nirari III reports that Jehoash paid him tribute, an event noted in the context of a description of the Assyrian king's defeat of the "ruler of Damascus" (probably Ben-hadad II):

> He received two thousand talents of silver, one thousand talents of copper, two thousand talents of iron, three thousand multi-coloured garments and (plain) linen garments as tribute from Mari' of the land of Damascus. He received the tribute of Joash of Samaria, of the Tyrians and of the Sidonians (*Iraq* 35[1973]143).

In other texts (see *ANET* 281-82; *ARAB* I §§ 734-35, 739-40), this Assyrian humiliation of Damascus is dated to Adad-nirari's fifth year (806-805). According to the Assyrian eponym list, Adad-nirari campaigned against Arpad in his fifth year, so it is possible that he reached Damascus also. Payment of tribute in this year by Jehoash would mean that he was acting on behalf of the injured Jehoahaz. The payment may have occurred, however, in the following year. Adad nirari's Rimah inscription reports a campaign to the west in the first person and then describes his victory over Syria and Jehoash's payment of tribute in the third person, which suggests that the inscription is composite. The year 805-804 would certainly seem the most likely time for the Assyrian ruler to note the payment by Jehoash. Even Jehoahaz may have earlier paid tribute to Assyria, to his "savior" (2 Kings 13:5). Adad-nirari noted Jehoash's payment since it was his first tribute, made near the time Jehoash assumed the throne. It was the first payment in what must have been an annual affair as long as Assyria displayed strength. That the payment of tribute by Jehoash and the defeat of Ben-hadad occurred in Adad-nirari's sixth year (805-804) is also suggested but not required by the fact that Ben-hadad was apparently on the throne in Damascus in that year. If Hazael, who was apparently still reigning in his thirty-seventh year (807-806), had been king, the Assyrians would surely have named this well-known ruler. Presumably a new king had recently assumed control in Damascus.

In Judah, Amaziah succeeded to the throne, replacing his injured father Jehoash, on 15 Tishri 802, just before the beginning of the Israelite Jehoash's third year (2 Kings 14:1). Amaziah proved himself an aggressive ruler once he had solidified his hold on the throne. He took vengeance on his father's assailants (2 Kings 14:5) and won a decisive victory over the Edomites (2 Kings 14:7). Moving to assert Judean independence from renewed Israelite domination, he challenged Jehoash, but was roundly defeated (2 Kings 14:8-12). Amaziah was captured in battle at Beth-shemesh and was brought or came with Jehoash (reading the *ketib* rather than the *qere*) to Jerusalem where Jehoash demolished part of the city's fortifications and looted the temple and royal treasuries (2 Kings 14:13-14). Taking additional hostages, Jehoash returned to Samaria with Amaziah. The date of this Israelite victory cannot be established. It probably occurred shortly before Jehoash's death sometime after 15 Marheshvan 789, in the fourteenth year of Amaziah. Amaziah never regained the throne of Judah although he lived for fifteen years after Jehoash's death (2 Kings 14:17).

The date of Amaziah's release from Samaria cannot be determined, although it must have been after 785, when the people of Judah installed the sixteen-year old Azariah (Uzziah) on the throne (2 Kings 14:21). 2 Kings 14:19 reports that a conspiracy was hatched against Amaziah in Jerusalem, and he fled to Lachish where he was put to death (2 Kings 14:19-20). Amaziah, the strong nationalist, must have been plotting to regain the throne from Azariah whose policy was one of subordination to Israel and Jeroboam II.

7. FROM JEROBOAM II TO MENAHEM

JUDAH

AMAZIAH (802-786[774])

(15. Tishri 788 - Tishri 787)
(16. Tishri 787 - Tishri 786)
(17. Tishri 786 - ....)

AZARIAH(Uzziah) (785-760[734]) (Amaziah)

0. .... - Tishri 785
1. Tishri 785 - Tishri 784 (18)
2. Tishri 784 - Tishri 783 (19)
3. Tishri 783 - Tishri 782 (20)

4. Tishri 782 - Tishri 781 (21)
5. Tishri 781 - Tishri 780 (22)
6. Tishri 780 - Tishri 779 (23)
7. Tishri 779 - Tishri 778 (24)
8. Tishri 778 - Tishri 777 (25)
9. Tishri 777 - Tishri 776 (26)
10. Tishri 776 - Tishri 775 (27)
11. Tishri 775 - Tishri 774 (28)
12. Tishri 774 - Tishri 773 (29)
13. Tishri 773 - Tishri 772

ISRAEL

JEROBOAM II (788-748)

0. .... - Marheshvan 788
1. Marheshvan 788 - Marheshvan 787
2. Marheshvan 787 - Marheshvan 786
3. Marheshvan 786 - Marheshvan 785
4. Marheshvan 785 - Marheshvan 784
5. Marheshvan 784 - Marheshvan 783
6. Marheshvan 783 - Marheshvan 782

7. Marheshvan 782 - Marheshvan 781
8. Marheshvan 781 - Marheshvan 780
9. Marheshvan 780 - Marheshvan 779
10. Marheshvan 779 - Marheshvan 778
11. Marheshvan 778 - Marheshvan 777
12. Marheshvan 777 - Marheshvan 776
13. Marheshvan 776 - Marheshvan 775
14. Marheshvan 775 - Marheshvan 774
15. Marheshvan 774 - Marheshvan 773
16. Marheshvan 773 - Marheshvan 772

ASSYRIA

ADAD-NIRARI III (810-783)

23. Nisan 788 - Nisan 787
24. Nisan 787 - Nisan 786
25. Nisan 786 - Nisan 785

26. Nisan 785 - Nisan 784
27. Nisan 784 - Nisan 783
28. Nisan 783 - ....

SHALMANESER IV (782-7?)

0. .... - Nisan 782
1. Nisan 782 - Nisan 781
2. Nisan 781 - Nisan 780
3. Nisan 780 - Nisan 779
4. Nisan 779 - Nisan 778
5. Nisan 778 - Nisan 777
6. Nisan 777 - Nisan 776
7. Nisan 776 - Nisan 775
8. Nisan 775 - Nisan 774
9. Nisan 774 - Nisan 773
10. Nisan 773 - ....

ASHUR-DAN III (772-755)

0. .... - Nisan 772
1. Nisan 772 - Nisan 771
2. Nisan 771 - Nisan 770
3. Nisan 770 - Nisan 769
4. Nisan 769 - Nisan 768
5. Nisan 768 - Nisan 767
6. Nisan 767 - Nisan 766
7. Nisan 766 - Nisan 765
8. Nisan 765 - Nisan 764
9. Nisan 764 - Nisan 763
10. Nisan 763 - Nisan 762
11. Nisan 762 - Nisan 761
12. Nisan 761 - Nisan 760
13. Nisan 760 - Nisan 759

14. Nisan 759 - Nisan 758
15. Nisan 758 - Nisan 757
16. Nisan 757 - Nisan 756
17. Nisan 756 - Nisan 755
18. Nisan 755 - ....

---

17. Marheshvan 772 - Marheshvan 771
18. Marheshvan 771 - Marheshvan 770
19. Marheshvan 770 - Marheshvan 769
20. Marheshvan 769 - Marheshvan 768
21. Marheshvan 768 - Marheshvan 767
22. Marheshvan 767 - Marheshvan 766
23. Marheshvan 766 - Marheshvan 765
24. Marheshvan 765 - Marheshvan 764
25. Marheshvan 764 - Marheshvan 763
26. Marheshvan 763 - Marheshvan 762
27. Marheshvan 762 - Marheshvan 761
28. Marheshvan 761 - Marheshvan 760
29. Marheshvan 760 - Marheshvan 759

30. Marheshvan 759 - Marheshvan 758
31. Marheshvan 758 - Marheshvan 757
32. Marheshvan 757 - Marheshvan 756
33. Marheshvan 756 - Marheshvan 755
34. Marheshvan 755 - Marheshvan 754

---

14. Tishri 772 - Tishri 771
15. Tishri 771 - Tishri 770
16. Tishri 770 - Tishri 769
17. Tishri 769 - Tishri 768
18. Tishri 768 - Tishri 767
19. Tishri 767 - Tishri 766
20. Tishri 766 - Tishri 765
21. Tishri 765 - Tishri 764
22. Tishri 764 - Tishri 763
23. Tishri 763 - Tishri 762
24. Tishri 762 - Tishri 761
25. Tishri 761 - Tishri 760
26. Tishri 760 - ....

JOTHAM (759-744)

(Azariah)

0. .... - Tishri 759
1. Tishri 759 - Tishri 758   (27)
2. Tishri 758 - Tishri 757   (28)
3. Tishri 757 - Tishri 756   (29)
4. Tishri 756 - Tishri 755   (30)
5. Tishri 755 - Tishri 754   (31)

6. Tishri 754 - Tishri 753
7. Tishri 753 - Tishri 752
8. Tishri 752 - Tishri 751
9. Tishri 751 - Tishri 750
10. Tishri 750 - Tishri 749
11. Tishri 749 - Tishri 748
12. Tishri 748 - Tishri 747

13. Tishri 747 - Tishri 746

(32) 35. Marheshvan 754 - Marheshvan 753
(33) 36. Marheshvan 753 - Marheshvan 752
(34) 37. Marheshvan 752 - Marheshvan 751
(35) 38. Marheshvan 751 - Marheshvan 750
(36) 39. Marheshvan 750 - Marheshvan 749
(37) 40. Marheshvan 749 - Marheshvan 748
(38) 41. Marheshvan 748 - . . . .
     ZECHARIAH (6 months)

(39) SHALLUM (1 month)

ASHUR-NIRARI V (754-745)

0. . . . . - Nisan 754
1. Nisan 754 - Nisan 753
2. Nisan 753 - Nisan 752
3. Nisan 752 - Nisan 751
4. Nisan 751 - Nisan 750
5. Nisan 750 - Nisan 749
6. Nisan 749 - Nisan 748
7. Nisan 748 - Nisan 747

8. Nisan 747 - Nisan 746

9. Nisan 746 - Nisan 745
10. Nisan 745 - . . . .

7. From Jeroboam II to Menahem

M. **Cogan,** "Tyre and Tiglath-Pileser III: Chronological Notes," *JCS* 25(1973)96-99; W. W. **Hallo,** "From Qarqar to Carchemish: Assyria and Israel in the Light of New Discoveries," *BA* 23(1960)34-61 = *BAR* II (Garden City: Anchor Books, 1964)152-88; L. D. **Levine,** *Two Neo-Assyrian Stelae from Iran* (Toronto: Royal Ontario Museum, 1972); **Levine,** "Menahem and Tiglath-Pileser: A New Synchronism," *BASOR* 206(1972)40-42; N. **Na'aman,** "Historical and Chronological Notes on the Kingdoms of Israel and Judah in the Eighth Century B.C.," *VT* 36(1986)71-92; W. H. **Shea,** "The Date and Significance of the Samaria Ostraca," *IEJ* 27(1977)16-27; **Shea,** "Menahem and Tiglath-Pileser III," *JNES* 37(1978)43-50; H. **Tadmor,** "Azriyau of Yaudi," *SH* 8(1961)232-71; M. **Weippert,** "Menahem von Israel und seine Zeitgenossen in einer Steleninschrift des assyrischen Königs Tiglathpileser III. aus dem Iran, "*ZDPV* 89(1973)26-53.

Jeroboam II came to the throne in the fifteenth year of Amaziah, after 15 Tishri 788, and began a rule that lasted forty-one years, until sometime in Nisan 747 (2 Kings 14:23). Unfortunately, no reference to him appears in any known non-biblical inscription, although the fate of Israel during his reign closely paralleled that of Assyria. He continued the aggressive policy of Jehoash against Syria (2 Kings 13:24-25). While Assyria was strong, in the early years of his reign, until about the mid 760s, Israel was strong and recouped previously held territory in Galilee and Transjordan (2 Kings 14:25). Azariah benefitted from Jeroboam's rule, no doubt serving in a supportive, subordinate capacity. During Jeroboam's reign (after the death of the Israelite Jehoash, the king whose death is mentioned in 2 Kings 14:22), Azariah was able to reestablish Judean shipping at Elath, now recovered from Syrian control (2 Kings 14:22). He thus shared in the results of "how Jeroboam recovered for Judah in Israel [territory claimed or dominated by] Damascus and Hamath" (2 Kings 14:28). After the waning of Assyrian power under Ashur-dan III (772-755), the aggressive intervention of Urartu under Saduri II (about 764-734) in the politics of the eastern Mediterranean seaboard, and the formation of a strong anti-Assyrian coalition in the west, Jeroboam died holding securely only the Ephraimite hill country and a few beachheads in Galilee and Transjordan (see Hos. 1:4-5; Amos 1-2; 6:13-14; Isa. 9:1). For the last three years of his reign, a rival Israelite king, Pekah, supported by Syria and favoring an anti-Assyrian stance, competed with Jeroboam for the loyalty of the Israelites. 2 Kings 15:27 correctly dates Pekah's takeover in Samaria--"In the fifty-second year of Azariah king of Judah, Pekah son of Remaliah became king over Israel in Samaria" (734)--and correctly reports his total length of reign--"twenty years."

Second Kings 15:1 contains a synchronism with Jeroboam's reign--"in the twenty-seventh year of Jeroboam, Azariah began to reign"--which appears totally enigmatic. The figure cannot be the result of the final editorial effort at synchronism since it appears impossible in light of 2 Kings 14:17, 21, and 23. The only approach that makes any sense of this twenty-seventh year of Jeroboam (762-761) is to assume that it originally referred to the year in which Azariah was struck with "leprosy," forcing him to turn over administrative authority to his son Jotham and eventually to give up the throne entirely (two years later, in 760-759; 2 Kings 15:5).

Jotham succeeded his father Azariah in Jerusalem at the fall festival of 759. Unfortunately, the synchronisms of the Judean kings, Jotham (2 Kings 15:32) and Ahaz (2 Kings 16:1), are correlated with the reign of Pekah, whose twenty years the editors thought had to be fitted between Pekahiah and Hoshea. The editors inherited sources which correctly synchronized Pekah's takeover in Samaria with Azariah's fifty-second year (734) and assigned Pekah twenty years (2 Kings 15:27). Assuming that Azariah's fifty-second year was his last year of actual rule rather than the year of his death, the editor's produced synchronisms between Pekah and the Judean successors to Azariah on this basis. 2 Kings 15:32 and 16:1 reflect these calculations (compare 17:1). These two synchronisms are therefore useless for chronological reconstruction and must be ignored. Fortunately, synchronisms between Judah and Israel using Judah as the base reference for the final years of Israel are correct except for 2 Kings 15:30.

Before his death, Jeroboam's reign and that of the house of Jehu were placed under the strongest scrutiny and denunciation by the prophets Hosea and Amos. The former appeared on the scene a few years before the death of Jeroboam, perhaps about 752, since the birth and nursing period of Gomer's first child occurred in the

final years of Jeroboam (Hos. 1:2-5). Amos carried out his preaching ministry shortly thereafter, about 750-749, two years before the
earthquake that devastated Palestine (see Amos 1:1; Zech. 14:5; and
Isa. 9:8-12, which mentions the earthquake before describing the
assassination of Zechariah and the killing of Shallum in vv. 13-17).
This earthquake, probably in the twelfth year of Jotham and the
forty-first year of Jeroboam II (748-747), marked the beginning of
Isaiah's career (Isa. 1:1) and was referred to in his early preaching
(see Isa. 1:2-20; 2:6-22).

Jeroboam died in Nisan 747. His son Zechariah succeeded
him, reigning six months or until about mid-Tishri. This was in the
thirty-eighth year of Azariah (2 Kings 14:29; 15:8). Shallum, supported by the general population, attacked Zechariah and killed him,
just after 15 Tishri 747, in the thirty-ninth year of Azariah (2 Kings
15:10). Shallum was undoubtedly the leader of a strong anti-
Assyrian faction with widespread support in both Israel and Judah.
After ruling "a month of days" (2 Kings 15:13b), in fact probably until
15 Marheshvan 747, Shallum was prevented by Israelite leaders from
participation in the anointment ritual. Menahem and his troops
moved to Samaria from Tirzah, attacked Shallum, and killed him (2
Kings 15:14). Menahem then assumed the kingship in Samaria in
the thirty-ninth year of Azariah (2 Kings 15:17), but because he
arrived in Samaria after 15 Marheshvan, his first regnal year did not
begin until the next fall festival, in 746. Thus the year 747-746 went
unattributed to any Israelite king.

8. FROM MENAHEM TO THE FIRST CAPTURE OF SAMARIA

JUDAH

JOTHAM (759-744)

14. Tishri 746 - Tishri 745
15. Tishri 745 - Tishri 744
16. Tishri 744 - ....

JEHOAHAZ I (743-728)

	(Azariah)
0. .... - Tishri 743	
1. Tishri 743 - Tishri 742	(40)
2. Tishri 742 - Tishri 741	(41)
3. Tishri 741 - Tishri 740	(42)
4. Tishri 740 - Tishri 739	(43)
5. Tishri 739 - Tishri 738	(44)
6. Tishri 738 - Tishri 737	(45)
7. Tishri 737 - Tishri 736	(46)
8. Tishri 736 - Tishri 735	(47)
9. Tishri 735 - Tishri 734	(48)
10. Tishri 734 - Tishri 733	(49)
11. Tishri 733 - Tishri 732	(50)
12. Tishri 732 - Tishri 731	(51)
13. Tishri 731 - Tishri 730	(52)

ISRAEL

MENAHEM (746-737)

0. .... - Marheshvan 746
1. Marheshvan 746 - Marheshvan 745
2. Marheshvan 745 - Marheshvan 744
3. Marheshvan 744 - Marheshvan 743
4. Marheshvan 743 - Marheshvan 742
5. Marheshvan 742 - Marheshvan 741
6. Marheshvan 741 - Marheshvan 740
7. Marheshvan 740 - Marheshvan 739
8. Marheshvan 739 - Marheshvan 738
9. Marheshvan 738 - Marheshvan 737
10. Marheshvan 737 - ....

PEKAHIAH (736-735)

0. .... - Marheshvan 736
1. Marheshvan 736 - Marheshvan 735
2. Marheshvan 735 - ....

PEKAH (734-731)

0. .... - Marheshvan 734
1. Marheshvan 734 - Marheshvan 733
2. Marheshvan 733 - Marheshvan 732
3. Marheshvan 732 - Marheshvan 731
4. Marheshvan 731 - ....

ASSYRIA

TIGLATH-PILESER III (744-727)

0. 13 Iyyar 744 - Nisan 744
1. Nisan 744 - Nisan 743
2. Nisan 743 - Nisan 742
3. Nisan 742 - Nisan 741
4. Nisan 741 - Nisan 740
5. Nisan 740 - Nisan 739
6. Nisan 739 - Nisan 738
7. Nisan 738 - Nisan 737
8. Nisan 737 - Nisan 736
9. Nisan 736 - Nisan 735
10. Nisan 735 - Nisan 734
11. Nisan 734 - Nisan 733
12. Nisan 733 - Nisan 732
13. Nisan 732 - Nisan 731
14. Nisan 731 - Nisan 730

14. Tishri 730 - Tishri 729
15. Tishri 729 - Tishri 728
16. Tishri 728 - ....

HEZEKIAH (727-699)
0. .... - Tishri 727
1. Tishri 727 - Tishri 726

2. Tishri 726 - Tishri 725
3. Tishri 725 - Tishri 724
4. Tishri 724 - Tishri 723
5. Tishri 723 - Tishri 722
6. Tishri 722 - Tishri 721

HOSHEA (730-722)
0. .... - Marheshvan 730
1. Marheshvan 730 - Marheshvan 729
2. Marheshvan 729 - Marheshvan 728
3. Marheshvan 728 - Marheshvan 727

4. Marheshvan 727 - Marheshvan 726

5. Marheshvan 726 - Marheshvan 725
6. Marheshvan 725 - Marheshvan 724
7. Marheshvan 724 - Marheshvan 723
8. Marheshvan 723 - Marheshvan 722
9. Marheshvan 722 - ....

15. Nisan 730 - Nisan 729
16. Nisan 729 - Nisan 728
17. Nisan 728 - Nisan 727

18. Nisan 727 - Tebet (727)

SHALMANESER V (726-722)
0. 25 Tebet - Nisan 726
1. Nisan 726 - Nisan 725
2. Nisan 725 - Nisan 724
3. Nisan 724 - Nisan 723
4. Nisan 723 - Nisan 722
5. Nisan 722 - Tebet (722)

8. From Menahem to the First Capture of Samaria

A. **Alt**, "Tiglathpilesers III. erster Feldzug nach Palästina," *Kleine Schriften zur Geschichte des Volkes Israel, II* (Munich: C. H. Beck, 1953)150-62; J. M. **Asurmendi,** *La Guerra Siro-Efraimita: Historia y Profetas* (Valencia/Jerusalem: Institución San Jerónimo, 1982); W. H. **Barnes,** *Studies in the Chronology of the Divided Monarchy of Israel* (dissertation, Harvard University, 1986)169-74; J. **Begrich,** "Der syrisch-emphraimitische Krieg und seine weltpolitischen Zusammenhänge," *ZDMG* 83(1929)213-37 = his *Gesammelte Studien* (Munich: Chr. Kaiser, 1964)99-120; R. **Borger** and H. **Tadmor,** "Zwei Beiträge zur alttestamentlichen Wissenschaft aufgrund der Inschriften Tiglatpilesers III," *ZAW* 94(1982)244-51; H. **Cazelles,** "Problemes de la guerre Syro-Ephraimite," *EI* 14(1978)70-78; H. J. **Cook,** "Pekah," *VT* 14(1964)121-35; H. **Donner,** *Israel unter den Völkern. Die Stellung der klassischen Propheten des 8. Jahrhunderts v. Chr. zur Aussenpolitik der Könige von Israel und Juda* (Leiden: E. J. Brill, 1964); M. **Elat,** "The Economic Relations of the Neo-Assyrian Empire with Egypt," *JAOS* 98(1978)20-34; S. H. **Horn,** "The Chronology of King Hezekiah's Reign," *AUSS* 2(1964)40-52; N. **Na'aman,** "The Brook of Egypt and Assyrian Policy on the Border of Egypt," *TA* 6(1976)68-90; B. **Oded,** "The Historical Background of the Syro-Ephraimite War Reconsidered," *CBQ* 34(1972)153-65; H. W. F. **Saggs,** "The Nimrud Letters, 1952--Part II," *Iraq* 17(1955)126-54; C. S. **Shaw,** "Micah 1:10-16 Reconsidered," *JBL* 106(1987)223-29; G. **Smith,** "On a New Fragment of the Assyrian Canon Belonging to the Reigns of Tiglath-pileser and Shalmaneser," *TSBA* 2(1873)321-32; H. **Tadmor,** "The Southern Border of Aram," *IEJ* 12(1962)114-22; **Tadmor,** "Philistia under Assyrian Rule," *BA* 29(1966)86-102; **Tadmor,** "Introductory Remarks to a New Edition of the Annals of Tiglath-Pileser III," *Proceedings of the Israel Academy of Sciences and Humanities* II/9(1967)168-87; **Tadmor** and M. **Cogan,** "Ahaz and Tiglath-pileser in the Book of Kings: Historiographic Considerations," *Biblica* 60(1979)491-508; E. **Vogt,** "Die Texte Tiglat-Pilesers III. über die Eroberung Palästinas," *Biblica* 45(1964)348-54; D. J. **Wiseman,** "Two Historical Inscriptions from Nimrud," *Iraq* 13(1951)21-26; **Wiseman,** "A Fragmentary Inscription of Tiglath-pileser III from Nimrud," *Iraq* 18(1956)117-29.

Menahem assumed the throne in Marheshvan 747, a few days less than eighteen months before Tiglath-pileser came to the throne in Assyria on 13 Iyyar 745 and began his move to reassert Assyrian authority throughout the Fertile Crescent. Internal and external pressure on Menahem early in his reign must have been enormous. In fact, he was able to retain the throne only through aggressive and brutal actions (2 Kings 15:16). A majority of the Israelites probably favored the rival king Pekah and supported joining the Urartian-inspired anti-Assyrian coalition, now led in Syria-Palestine by the Syrian king Rezin. Rezin undoubtedly had dreams of reestablishing the old empire of Hazael. Even before the death of Jeroboam II, "Syrians on the east and the Philistines on the west had devoured Israel with open mouth" (Isa. 9:12; see 2 Chron. 28:18). Early in his reign, before the Assyrians reappeared in the west in strength, Menahem had lost all control over "the way of the sea, the land beyond Jordan, and Galilee of the nations" (Isa. 9:1b) and was left with only the rump state of Ephraim as his domain.

Jotham, now in his last years, adhered to Menahem's policy of continued reliance on Assyria, and paid the price for his adherence. Many Judean cities, especially in the Shephelah where Philistine pressure was strong, apparently sided with the anti-Assyrian coalition (see Micah 1-2). Rezin and Pekah, acting in concert, harassed Judah (2 Kings 15:37), probably gaining dominance over all of Transjordan where Jotham had earlier exercised some cooperative control with Jeroboam II (1 Chron. 5:1-17). Whether Judah lost control of Elath and its outlet to the Red Sea under Jotham or under Ahaz remains uncertain; at any rate it was soon brought back under Syrian control as it had been during the days of Hazael (2 Kings 16:6). The Edomites cooperated with and benefited from Rezin's takeover of Elath and themselves encroached on Judean territory (2 Chron. 28:17).

In 743, Tiglath-pileser was able to turn his attention to the west and began a campaign there that lasted four years. While his attention focused primarily on northern Syria where Urartian influence was strongest, he seems to have campaigned widely in the eastern Mediterranean seaboard. He intervened in Israelite affairs, either going himself or sending an expeditionary force into the country. Assyrian military aid allowed Menahem to stabilize his control on the throne, but it was aid that came with a high price and required heavy taxation on Menaham's subjects, Judeans included (2 Kings 15:20-21; see Hos. 5:13; Isa. 3:16-4:1).

Menahem probably first paid tribute to Tiglath-pileser during the latter's presence in the west in 743-740. An Assyrian inscription, recently discovered in Iran, reports on the payment of tribute by several rulers in Syria-Palestine: Rezin of Damascus, Menahem of Samaria, Tubail of Tyre, Sibittibi'li (or Sibatbail) of Byblos, and Zabibe, queen of Arabia (Levine 19). That Tubail (= the Tabeel of Isa. 7:6) was on the throne at the time in Tyre suggests a date in the late 740s, since he had been succeeded by Hiram by 738.

Tiglath-pileser was back in the west in 738, after a short absence, and later noted in his annals the receipt of tribute from a number of western rulers including Rezin of Damascus, Menahem of Samaria, Hiram of Tyre, Sibittibi'li of Byblos, Pisiris of Carchemish, and Zabibe, the queen of Arabia (*ANET* 283; *ARAB* I § 772).

In Judah, Jotham had died after 15 Tishri 744, before Tiglath-pileser's first campaign to the west, after a reign of sixteen years (2 Kings 15:33). His synchronism with the reign of Pekah in 2 Kings 15:32 is useless as a reference point since the editors placed Pekah's entire twenty-year reign after that of Pekahiah. The reference to Jotham's twentieth year as the date of Hoshea's assumption of the throne in Samaria in 2 Kings 15:30 makes no sense whatever in light of 2 Kings 15:32-33. It does not appear, however, to be a late editorial synchronism since it does not synchronize with any other calculations. The statement is probably a misreading of a source that originally referred to Hoshea's accession to the throne in a twentieth year, but with reference to Pekah, not Jotham (see 2 Kings 15:27).

Jehoahaz I (Ahaz) succeeded his father Jotham in 744-743. The pro-Assyrian stance of Menahem in Israel would have been policy of state for Ahaz although there is no evidence to indicate that Ahaz conducted direct negotiations with Assyria (see Hos. 5:13). As had been the case throughout the years of the Jehu dynasty, Judah related to Assyria via Israel to whom the south played a subordinate, vassal role. As we noted, Judah probably shared in the cost of Menahem's tribute to Tiglath-pileser (2 Kings 15:19-20). Facing growing internal opposition, especially from the upper, tribute-paying class, and the disaffection of many Judean cities and citizens (the "this people" of Isaiah 6-8), Ahaz probably sought to gain support among the lower classes of Jerusalem and Judah. The so-called Book of the Covenant (Exod. 21:1-23:19) with its concern for justice in society and its regulations on behalf of the unprivileged classes was probably proclaimed as a social reformation document or royal *misharum* at the fall festival in either 742 or 735. (Note Isaiah's depiction of Ahaz in Isa. 11:1-6.)

Menahem died after 15 Tishri 736, the beginning of Azariah's fiftieth year (2 Kings 15:23). His son Pekahiah succeeded him and was anointed on 15 Marheshvan 736. Pekahiah reigned for only two years before being attacked and killed by Pekah (2 Kings 15:25). Pekah's takeover of the throne in Samaria must have occurred between 15 Tishri (the beginning of Azariah's fifty-second year; 2 Kings 15:27) and 15 Marheshvan 734, making 734 Pekah's first regnal year in Samaria. Azariah apparently died shortly after 15 Tishri 734 (see Isa. 6:1).

With Pekah's assumption of the throne, Israel threw its support behind the anti-Assyrian coalition. Ahaz was expected to go along as a loyal vassal to Israel, and the Judeans as a whole supported such a move (Isa. 8:6). Ahaz, encouraged by Isaiah (all of Isaiah 6-12 belongs to this crisis, as does Micah 3-5), declared his independence from Israelite policy (note especially Isa. 9:2) and his unwillingness to participate in the coalition. Ahaz and Jerusalem were left isolated in the southern Syro-Palestinian world.

After an attempted assassination of Ahaz failed (2 Chron. 28:7), Pekah and Rezin decided on a blitzkrieg to Jerusalem in order to remove Ahaz from the throne and replace Davidic rule with a "son of Tabeel," a prince from the royal house of Tyre (Isa. 7:6). The Syro-Ephraimitic march to Jerusalem (Isa. 10:27d-32) must have been made sometime after 15 Marheshvan 734. The city was placed under siege.

The plans of Pekah and Rezin to depose the house of David were interrupted by the appearance of Tiglath-pileser on the scene late in 734 or early in 733. According to the Assyrian eponym list, the king conducted a campaign to Philistia between Nisan 734 and Nisan 733, probably late in the year since 735-734 was spent in the east against Urartu. The Assyrian king had come west at his first opportunity. The preceding four years had been spent in campaigns to the north and east.

Between 15 Tishri 734 and Nisan 733, a number of momentous events occurred: the aged and apparently highly venerated patriarch Azariah (Uzziah) died; Isaiah had his famous temple vision and moved into the center of Judean politics; with Syrian encouragement, Pekah seized the throne in Samaria and declared the state's support for the anti-Assyrian coalition; Ahaz proclaimed Judean independence from Israel; an attempt to assassinate Ahaz failed; Rezin and Pekah moved to topple the Davidic house, placing Jerusalem under siege; Tiglath-pileser arrived in the west and moved down the Mediterranean coast, his presence in the area forcing the withdrawal of Ephraimite and Syrian forces from Jerusalem.

Assyrian operations in the west against the coalition lasted three years (734-733, 733-732, and 732-731). That Tiglath-pileser came west merely to rescue Ahaz and that Ahaz secured Assyrian help by sending tribute (2 Kings 16:7-9) are the products of later editors. Ahaz was simply the beneficiary of Tiglath-pileser's initial move against the coalition. Like other rulers, mostly submissive rebels, Ahaz paid tribute after Tiglath-pileser's 734-733 campaign.

Several Assyrian texts, all fragmentary, describe Tiglath-pileser's three year struggle with the western anti-Assyrian coalition. In the first phase, the campaign to Philistia (late 734 or early 733), Tiglath-pileser moved quickly down the Mediterranean coast, suppressed the Philistine rebels, fought the Meunites in the region south of Gaza, established an Assyrian commercial center in the city or region of Gaza, and set up his royal image at the Brook of Egypt (at this time, Wadi Besor) (see ND 400 in Wiseman [1951]23-24; Borger-Tadmor 250). The purposes of this campaign were (1) to strike suddenly and quickly bring to submission as many of the coastal powers as possible, (2) to reassert Assyrian authority in Mediterranean and Arab trade, and (3) to block any Egyptian/Ethiopian move to aid the Syro-Palestinian rebels. The list of rulers paying tribute at the time (reported in II R 67 rev. 7-12; see *ANET* 282; *ARAB* I §§ 800-801) included Jehoahaz (Ahaz) of Judah. Missing from this list are the three dominant powers in the anti-Assyrian coalition, namely, Rezin of Damascus, Hiram of Tyre, and Pekah of Israel.

In his second and third campaigns (against Damascus; 733-732, 732-731), Tiglath-pileser broke the back of the rebellion, captured Damascus, killed Rezin (according to 2 Kings 16:9), defeated the other allies (including Samsi, queen of Arabia), and provincialized the territory (sixteen districts) held by Damascus including Transjordan, Galilee, and the Palestinian coastal plain between Philistia and Phoenicia (see 2 Kings 15:29; 1 Chron. 5:26).

Assyrian actions related to Israel during this period and bearing on chronological issues suggest the following course of events and

Israel's somewhat subordinate role in the revolt. (1) Israelite troops certainly engaged in warfare with Assyria. There may have been some fighting in Ephraimite territory, which was all that remained of the Israelite state (unless one counts whatever territory Pekah held under Syrian overlordship prior to his coup in Samaria in 734). Tiglath-pileser claims to have deported people and carried away spoils and tribute from Omri-land. (2) Samaria, the old territory held by Menahem, was left intact as a political entity. None of this territory was taken over by the Assyrians. (3) Hoshea was recognized by Tiglath-pileser as the new ruler of Samaria (*ANET* 283-84; *ARAB* I §§ 779, 815-16).

Tiglath-pileser describes his role in Hoshea's takeover by noting that "they (the Ephraimites) overthrew their king Pekah and I placed Hoshea as king over them." In addition, the Assyrian text ND 4301 + 4305 (see Wiseman [1956]; Borger-Tadmor 244-49) reports that Hoshea sent tribute to Tiglath-pileser while the latter was fighting in southern Babylonia in 730. The biblical text also describes Hoshea's takeover, but without reference to the role of Tiglath-pileser (2 Kings 15:30; 17:1). 2 Kings 15:30 reports that Hoshea organized a conspiracy against Pekah, attacked him, and killed him (in Pekah's twentieth year?). 2 Kings 17:1 states that Hoshea began to rule in Ahaz's twelfth year (732-731).

We reconstruct the chronology of the events surrounding Hoshea's takeover as follows. During Tiglath-pileser's second campaign against Damascus (begun between Nisan 732 and Nisan 731), Israelite forces were defeated and some captives and spoils taken. During this campaign, Hoshea organized a countermovement against Pekah and was recognized and designated by Tiglath-pileser to succeed Pekah before the Assyrian king left Syria-Palestine, probably in the late spring or early summer of 731. Ahaz attended a meeting in Damascus, probably called for the purpose of setting up and confirming the new arrangements in Syria-Palestine sealed by vassal treaties of submission to Tiglath-pileser (2 Kings 16:10a).

Hoshea's recognition as king by a portion of the Ephraimite population and by the Assyrians thus occurred in the twelfth year of Ahaz, before 15 Tishri 731 (2 Kings 17:1). Like Jehu in 841-840, Hoshea still had to gain control of his kingdom. Pekah, who appears to have had widespread popular support both in his years as a rival king (750-734) and as reigning monarch in Samaria (734-731), was able to hold out in Samaria until after 15 Marheshvan 731. Thus several months of civil war and perhaps a preliminary siege of Samaria lie behind the statement that Hoshea attacked Pekah and put him to death (2 Kings 15:30). Hosea 6:11-7:7 may refer to the new year festival of 15 Marheshvan 731, shortly after which Pekah was deposed by (or at least his overthrow was aided by) Samaria's leaders. According to Tiglath-pileser, he was overthrown by his own subjects. By the time Hoshea stabilized control of Samaria and collected and dispatched tribute for Tiglath-pileser, the Assyrian king had begun his campaign into southern Babylonia (see Isaiah 13) and was engaged in the siege of Sarrabanu (ND 4301 + 4305).

Ahaz and Tiglath-pileser died within a few months of each other; Ahaz sometime before 15 Tishri 727 and Tiglath-pileser in Tebet 727 (Isa. 14:28-32). Two years before his death, in 729, Tiglath-pileser had suppressed a rebellion and assumed the kingship in Babylon (*ABC* 72-73; Isa. 14:1-27), becoming the first Assyrian monarch since Tiglath-pileser I (1115-1070) to reign as king in this old, revered, religious and cultural center.

Apparently before Tiglath-pileser's death, open rebellion had again erupted in the west. Indications of trouble are found in a Nimrud tablet from 729 which mentions the Assyrian replacement of an uncooperative king in Tabal and the forceful exaction of tribute from Tyre (*ANET* 282; *ARAB* I §§ 802-3). A fragment of an eponym list in the British Museum (see Smith) notes the following for Tiglath-pileser's final years:

> [728-727] Eponym Durasser governor of Tushan, the king
>   took the hand of Bel. The city Di. . .(broken).
> [727-726] Eponym Belharran-bel-uzur governor of Gozan,
>   expedition to the city of. . .(broken).
>   Shalmaneser sat on the throne.

The apparent reference to Damascus (*Di-mash-qa*) and a military campaign suggest that revolt had erupted in Damascus and other Syro-Palestinian states by 728-727 and the Assyrian king moved west to suppress the uprising, perhaps accompanied by Shalmaneser, his successor. The circumstances of Tiglath-pileser's death are unknown. The Babylonian Chronicles merely note that he died in the month Tebet (*ABC* 72). One could hypothesize on the basis of the eponym statements that he died on a campaign to the west (see Isa. 14:1-27).

Shalmaneser V succeeded Tiglath-pileser on 25 Tebet (*ABC* 73). For information about Shalmaneser's reign, we are dependent upon biblical texts, Josephus's *Antiquities* IX 283-87, where he quotes Menander's excerpts from Tyrian records, and the sketchy material in the eponym lists and the Babylonian Chronicles, since no Assyrian historical inscriptions of Shalmaneser are known. His reign is of great significance for the history of Israel since he presided over the final days of Samaria and captured the city before his death (*ABC* 73).

Three episodes in Samaria's last days are related to Shalmaneser. (1) He came up against Hoshea, presumably at a time when Samaria was in revolt, forced Hoshea's submission and payment of tribute, and subjected him to vassal status based on a vassal treaty (2 Kings 17:3). (2) Hoshea became disloyal again, appealed to Egypt for help, and was arrested and imprisoned by Shalmaneser (2 Kings 17:4). (3) At some later time, apparently with the city again in revolt, Shalmaneser invaded Ephraim in force, and besieged Samaria for three years, beginning in the seventh year of Hoshea and the fourth year of Hezekiah (2 Kings 18:9), before capturing the city in Hoshea's ninth (2 Kings 17:5-6) and Hezekiah's sixth year (2 Kings 18:10). Josephus reports that Shalmaneser came with an army and invaded Syria and all of Phoenicia and then, quoting Menander, describes the Assyrian action against Phoenicia, and Tyre in particular, as taking place in two phases. Shalmaneser's initial attack was followed by withdrawal from the region, after which he returned, placing Tyre under a siege that lasted five years. This evidence and the chronology are best understood in the following reconstruction.

727-726   Tiglath-pileser and Shalmaneser began a campaign to put down a rebellion in the west during which Tiglath-pileser died. Shalmaneser carried through on this campaign in his accession period but was not totally successful. Hoshea's first submission occurred during the period of Assyrian warfare against Moab and Damascus and the beginning of the Phoenician operation. (Isaiah 15-17 reflect this background; see Hos. 10:14.) Shalmaneser returned to Assyria for his coronation in Nisan 726.

726-725   Shalmaneser remained in Assyria and went on no campaign. During this year revolt erupted again in the west, and Hoshea, probably giving in to popular pressure, appealed to Egypt for help (2 Kings 17:4a), after Ethiopian ambassadors had visited Syria-Palestine (Isaiah 18). This phase of the struggle is reflected in Isaiah 28-32 and Hos. 7:11-16.

725-724   Shalmaneser returned to the west, at which time Hoshea was arrested, probably by Assyrian troops stationed in Samaria (see Isa. 28:11-13). The royal palace and sanctuary were destroyed and the royal cultic paraphenalia taken away (2 Kings 17:4b; Isaiah 32; Hos. 3; 8:1-10:15; Micah 6-7). Tyre was placed under siege until Sargon's first western campaign in 720.

724-723   Although Hoshea had been arrested, rebellion flamed anew in Ephraim and Samaria. Shalmaneser returned to the country (Isaiah 33) and placed Samaria under siege sometime shortly after 15 Marheshvan, in the fourth year of Hezekiah and the seventh year of Hoshea (2 Kings 17:5; 18:9). Hosea 11-14 belong to this and the following years.

723-722   The siege of Samaria continued.

722-(721)   The city of Samaria was taken by Shalmaneser between 15 Marheshvan, the beginning of Hoshea's ninth year (2 Kings 17:6), and 12 Tebet, when, after Shalmaneser's death, Sargon II ascended the throne (*ABC* 73).

9. FROM THE SECOND CAPTURE OF SAMARIA
TO THE RISE OF BABYLONIA

JUDAH	ASSYRIA
HEZEKIAH (727-699)	**SARGON II (721-705)**

	JUDAH		ASSYRIA
		0.	12 Tebet - Nisan 721
		1.	Nisan 721 - Nisan 720
7.	Tishri 721 - Tishri 720	2.	Nisan 720 - Nisan 719
8.	Tishri 720 - Tishri 719	3.	Nisan 719 - Nisan 718
9.	Tishri 719 - Tishri 718	4.	Nisan 718 - Nisan 717
10.	Tishri 718 - Tishri 717	5.	Nisan 717 - Nisan 716
11.	Tishri 717 - Tishri 716	6.	Nisan 716 - Nisan 715
12.	Tishri 716 - Tishri 715	7.	Nisan 715 - Nisan 714
13.	Tishri 715 - Tishri 714	8.	Nisan 714 - Nisan 713
14.	Tishri 714 - Tishri 713	9.	Nisan 713 - Nisan 712
15.	Tishri 713 - Tishri 712	10.	Nisan 712 - Nisan 711
16.	Tishri 712 - Tishri 711	11.	Nisan 711 - Nisan 710
17.	Tishri 711 - Tishri 710	12.	Nisan 710 - Nisan 709
18.	Tishri 710 - Tishri 709	13.	Nisan 709 - Nisan 708
19.	Tishri 709 - Tishri 708	14.	Nisan 708 - Nisan 707
20.	Tishri 708 - Tishri 707	15.	Nisan 707 - Nisan 706
21.	Tishri 707 - Tishri 706	16.	Nisan 706 - Nisan 705
22.	Tishri 706 - Tishri 705	17.	Nisan 705 - . . . .
23.	Tishri 705 - Tishri 704		

SENNACHERIB (704-681)

	JUDAH		ASSYRIA
		0.	12 Ab 705 - Nisan 704
		1.	Nisan 704 - Nisan 703
24.	Tishri 704 - Tishri 703	2.	Nisan 703 - Nisan 702
25.	Tishri 703 - Tishri 702	3.	Nisan 702 - Nisan 701
26.	Tishri 702 - Tishri 701	4.	Nisan 701 - Nisan 700
27.	Tishri 701 - Tishri 700	5.	Nisan 700 - Nisan 699
28.	Tishri 700 - Tishri 699	6.	Nisan 699 - Nisan 698
29.	Tishri 699 -		

MANASSEH (698-644)

	JUDAH		ASSYRIA
0.	. . . . - Tishri 698		
1.	Tishri 698 - Tishri 697	7.	Nisan 698 - Nisan 697
2.	Tishri 697 - Tishri 696	8.	Nisan 697 - Nisan 696
3.	Tishri 696 - Tishri 695	9.	Nisan 696 - Nisan 695
4.	Tishri 695 - Tishri 694	10.	Nisan 695 - Nisan 694
5.	Tishri 694 - Tishri 693	11.	Nisan 694 - Nisan 693
6.	Tishri 693 - Tishri 692	12.	Nisan 693 - Nisan 692
7.	Tishri 692 - Tishri 691	13.	Nisan 692 - Nisan 691
		14.	Nisan 691 - Nisan 690

8.	Tishri 691 - Tishri 690		15.	Nisan 690 - Nisan 689
9.	Tishri 690 - Tishri 689		16.	Nisan 689 - Nisan 688
10.	Tishri 689 - Tishri 688		17.	Nisan 688 - Nisan 687
11.	Tishri 688 - Tishri 687		18.	Nisan 687 - Nisan 686
12.	Tishri 687 - Tishri 686		19.	Nisan 686 - Nisan 685
13.	Tishri 686 - Tishri 685		20.	Nisan 685 - Nisan 684
14.	Tishri 685 - Tishri 684		21.	Nisan 684 - Nisan 683
15.	Tishri 684 - Tishri 683		22.	Nisan 683 - Nisan 682
16.	Tishri 683 - Tishri 682		23.	Nisan 682 - Nisan 681
17.	Tishri 682 - Tishri 681		24.	Nisan 681 - 20 Tebet

18. Tishri 681 - Tishri 680

ESARHADDON (680-669)

19.	Tishri 680 - Tishri 679		0.	8 Adar - Nisan 680
20.	Tishri 679 - Tishri 678		1.	Nisan 680 - Nisan 679
21.	Tishri 678 - Tishri 677		2.	Nisan 679 - Nisan 678
22.	Tishri 677 - Tishri 676		3.	Nisan 678 - Nisan 677
23.	Tishri 676 - Tishri 675		4.	Nisan 677 - Nisan 676
24.	Tishri 675 - Tishri 674		5.	Nisan 676 - Nisan 675
25.	Tishri 674 - Tishri 673		6.	Nisan 675 - Nisan 674
26.	Tishri 673 - Tishri 672		7.	Nisan 674 - Nisan 673
27.	Tishri 672 - Tishri 671		8.	Nisan 673 - Nisan 672
28.	Tishri 671 - Tishri 670		9.	Nisan 672 - Nisan 671
29.	Tishri 670 - Tishri 669		10.	Nisan 671 - Nisan 670
30.	Tishri 669 - Tishri 668		11.	Nisan 670 - Nisan 669
			12.	Nisan 669 - 10 Marheshvan

ASHURBANIPAL (668-627)

31.	Tishri 668 - Tishri 667		0.	.... - Nisan 668
32.	Tishri 667 - Tishri 666		1.	Nisan 668 - Nisan 667
33.	Tishri 666 - Tishri 665		2.	Nisan 667 - Nisan 666
34.	Tishri 665 - Tishri 664		3.	Nisan 666 - Nisan 665
35.	Tishri 664 - Tishri 663		4.	Nisan 665 - Nisan 664
36.	Tishri 663 - Tishri 662		5.	Nisan 664 - Nisan 663
37.	Tishri 662 - Tishri 661		6.	Nisan 663 - Nisan 662
38.	Tishri 661 - Tishri 660		7.	Nisan 662 - Nisan 661
39.	Tishri 660 - Tishri 659		8.	Nisan 661 - Nisan 660
40.	Tishri 659 - Tishri 658		9.	Nisan 660 - Nisan 659
41.	Tishri 658 - Tishri 657		10.	Nisan 659 - Nisan 658
42.	Tishri 657 - Tishri 656		11.	Nisan 658 - Nisan 657
43.	Tishri 656 - Tishri 655		12.	Nisan 657 - Nisan 656
44.	Tishri 655 - Tishri 654		13.	Nisan 656 - Nisan 655
			14.	Nisan 655 - Nisan 654
			15.	Nisan 654 - Nisan 653

45. Tishri 654 - Tishri 653
46. Tishri 653 - Tishri 652
47. Tishri 652 - Tishri 651
48. Tishri 651 - Tishri 650
49. Tishri 650 - Tishri 649
50. Tishri 649 - Tishri 648
51. Tishri 648 - Tishri 647
52. Tishri 647 - Tishri 646
53. Tishri 646 - Tishri 645
54. Tishri 645 - Tishri 644
55. Tishri 644 - . . . .

AMON (643-642)
0. . . . . - Tishri 643
1. Tishri 643 - Tishri 642
2. Tishri 642 - . . . .

JOSIAH (641-610)
0. . . . . - Tishri 641
1. Tishri 641 - Tishri 640
2. Tishri 640 - Tishri 639
3. Tishri 639 - Tishri 638
4. Tishri 638 - Tishri 637
5. Tishri 637 - Tishri 636
6. Tishri 636 - Tishri 635
7. Tishri 635 - Tishri 634
8. Tishri 634 - Tishri 633
9. Tishri 633 - Tishri 632
10. Tishri 632 - Tishri 631
11. Tishri 631 - Tishri 630
12. Tishri 630 - Tishri 629
13. Tishri 629 - Tishri 628
14. Tishri 628 - Tishri 627
15. Tishri 627 - Tishri 626
16. Tishri 626 - Tishri 625

16. Nisan 653 - Nisan 652
17. Nisan 652 - Nisan 651
18. Nisan 651 - Nisan 650
19. Nisan 650 - Nisan 649
20. Nisan 649 - Nisan 648
21. Nisan 648 - Nisan 647
22. Nisan 647 - Nisan 646
23. Nisan 646 - Nisan 645
24. Nisan 645 - Nisan 644
25. Nisan 644 - Nisan 643
26. Nisan 643 - Nisan 642

27. Nisan 642 - Nisan 641

28. Nisan 641 - Nisan 640
29. Nisan 640 - Nisan 639
30. Nisan 639 - Nisan 638
31. Nisan 638 - Nisan 637
32. Nisan 637 - Nisan 636
33. Nisan 636 - Nisan 635
34. Nisan 635 - Nisan 634
35. Nisan 634 - Nisan 633
36. Nisan 633 - Nisan 632
37. Nisan 632 - Nisan 631
38. Nisan 631 - Nisan 630
39. Nisan 630 - Nisan 629
40. Nisan 629 - Nisan 628
41. Nisan 628 - Nisan 627
42. Nisan 627 - . . . .

9. From the Second Capture of Samaria to the Rise of Babylonia

J. A. **Brinkman**, "Merodach-Baladan II," in *Studies Presented to A. Leo Oppenheim* (ed. R. D. Biggs and J. A. Brinkman; Chicago: Oriental Institute, 1964)6-53; R. **Frankena**, "The Vassal Treaties of Esarhaddon and the Dating of Deuteronomy," *OTS* 14(1965)122-54; C. J. **Gadd**, "Inscribed Prisms of Sargon II from Nimrud," *Iraq* 16(1954)173-201; L. D. **Levine**, "Sennacherib's Southern Front: 704-689 B. C.," *JCS* 34(1982)28-58; A. **Malamat**, "The Historical Background of the Assassination of Amon, King of Judah," *IEJ* 3(1953)26-29; N. **Na'aman**, "Sennacherib's 'Letter to God' on His Campaign to Judah," *BASOR* 214(1974)25-39; J. N. **Postgate**, "Assyrian Texts and Fragments: 5. Sargon's Letter Referring to Midas," *Iraq* 35(1973)21-34; J. E. **Reade**, "Sargon's Campaigns of 720, 716, and 715 B.C.: Evidence from the Sculptures," *JNES* 35(1976)95-104; D. G. **Schley**, Jr., "'Yahweh Will Cause You to Return to Egypt in Ships' (Deuteronomy XXVIII 68)," *VT* 35(1985)369-72; W. H. **Shea**, "Sennacherib's Second Palestinian Campaign," *JBL* 104(1985)401-18; A. **Spalinger**, "Assurbanipal and Egypt: A Source Study," *JAOS* 94(1974)316-28; **Spalinger**, "Esarhaddon and Egypt: An Analysis of the First Invasion of Egypt," *Or* 43(1974)295-326; **Spalinger**, "Psammetichus, King of Egypt: I," *JARCE* 13(1976)133-47; **Spalinger**, "Psammetichus, King of Egypt: II," *JARCE* 15(1978)49-57; **Spalinger**, "The Date of the Death of Gyges and Its Historical Implications," *JAOS* 98(1978)400-409; H. **Spieckermann**, *Juda unter Assur in der Sargonidenzeit* (Göttingen: Vandenhoeck and Ruprecht, 1982); H. **Tadmor**, "The Campaigns of Sargon II of Assur: A Chronological-Historical Study," *JCS* 12(1958)22-40, 77-100.

Hezekiah ascended the Judean throne following Ahaz's death (Isa. 14:28-32; 2 Kings 16:20) sometime after 15 Marheshvan 728, in the third year of Hoshea (2 Kings 18:1), and was officially installed on 15 Tishri 727. At the time, Tiglath-pileser (and probably Shalmaneser) was on campaign against a western anti-Assyrian revolt that involved several states including Moab (Isaiah 15-16), Damascus and Samaria (Isaiah 17; 2 Kings 17:3), Phoenicia (*Ant* IX 283-87), and probably Philistia (Isa. 14:28-32). Isaiah's ministry during this period concentrated on keeping Jerusalem and Judah out of the ranks of the anti-Assyrian coalition. (All of Isaiah 15-33 relates to the reign of Hezekiah, but in the following order: 15-18, 28-33, 19-27.)

Hezekiah had the option of participating in anti-Assyrian revolts on several occasions prior to the fall of Samaria but remained a loyal Assyrian vassal, presumably not even offering active assistance to Samaria during the state's final years.

All of Sargon II's reign (721-705) falls within the years of Hezekiah's rule. Sargon was a very active monarch and campaigned extensively. Early in his career he was concerned with domestic threats and trouble in the east where Merodach-baladan II (Marduk-apla-iddinna II) had laid claim to the throne of Babylon (*ABC* 73). His first contact with the west occurred in his second regnal year (720-719). After Shalmaneser's death, the western revolt continued and Sargon was confronted with opposition from Hamath to Gaza. Along with Hamath and Gaza, Arvad, Simirra, and Damascus, as well as Samaria, are noted as rebelling (*ANET* 284-85; *ARAB* II §§ 5, 55). That Samaria, which had been captured by Shalmaneser only two years earlier, was already striving for independence from Assyria, shows the depth of the popular anti-Assyrian sentiment which Pekah had embodied.

In an inscribed prism text from Calah, Sargon notes that the Samarians had given their allegiance to a king hostile to him (Gadd 179-80). It is uncertain whether this refers to the king of Hamath, the usurper Ia'ubidi whom Sargon captured and flayed, or, more likely, to a native Ephraimite who had taken the throne, either after the arrest of Hoshea (see Hos. 8:4) or after Shalmaneser's capture of the city.

Sargon refers to placing Samaria under siege, capturing the city, carrying away the gods of Samaria, deporting 27,280 people, provincializing the region, rebuilding the capital city, and settling foreigners there. Sargon is not taking credit here for the activities of Shalmaneser but describing his own actions taken in 720 and shortly thereafter. Thus we can expand the description of events and chronology surrounding the final days of Samaria given at the end of the last section. In 725-724, Shalmaneser had arrested and carried away King Hoshea and probably many of the country's leaders, destroyed the royal quarter in Samaria, and looted the royal sanctuary in Bethel. In the meantime, the citizens had refashioned their cultic artifacts, set these up in Samaria, and elevated a new ruler to lead them (see Hos. 13:2, 10). Shalmaneser breached the city walls but died before Samaria was fully transformed into an Assyrian province and further deportation of its citizens could take place. These tasks were left to Sargon. Thus 2 Kings 17:6 has combined the events surrounding the first and second captures of Samaria.

Sargon's 720 campaign took him to Philistia, where he defeated and captured Hanunu of Gaza, and to Raphia in Egyptian territory south of Wadi Besor. Raphia was destroyed, and a token Egyptian force probably sent by Osorkon IV (735-712), the last ruler of the XXIInd Dynasty, fled without offering much opposition (*ANET* 285; *ARAB* II § 55).

Two significant events resulted from Sargon's activity in southwest Palestine. First, Judah and Hezekiah, thoroughly cooperative with the Assyrians, probably contributed troops to the Assyrian military campaign. As a reward, Hezekiah was allowed to expand his territory in the southwest (1 Chron. 4:24-43; see Deut. 25:17-19). Second, Sargon inaugurated a new cooperative program between Assyria and the Egyptian princes in the Delta. (Both factors were celebrated in Isaiah's speech in chap. 19.) This policy is noted in the Calah Prism, where Sargon reports the following:

> I made the splendour of Ashur my lord overwhelm the Egyptians and Arabians. At the mention of my name their hearts trembled and their arms fell. The closed commercial center of Egypt I opened. The people of Assyria and Egypt I made mingle together and had them trade.

This commerical arrangement between Assyria and Egypt had as its goal the domination of trade in the eastern Mediterranean world. At the time, Anatolian states, Cyprus, Tyre, and the Greeks still conducted Mediterranean trade reasonably free from Assyrian control.

Insofar as politics in Egypt were concerned, Sargon's new policy allied Assyria with the Egyptian rulers of the Delta against the Ethiopians, the XXVth Egyptian Dynasty. The Ethiopian ruler Piye (about 753-713), who had claimed authority in all of Egypt throughout much of his early reign, had invaded northern Egypt in his twentieth year, shortly before or during Tiglath-pileser's campaigns against the western coalition (*AEL* III 66-84). After forc-

ing the submission of local rulers, he returned south but later sent
Ethiopian ambassadors into Syria-Palestine (Isaiah 18).

Later, with Sargon's new initiative in the area, the Delta princes
came under Assyrian influence. When Sargon was back in the west
in 716-715, he received a gift of twelve fine horses from an Egyptian
ruler in the Delta, called Shilkanni, apparently either Osorkon IV or
Bocchoris (718-712). With Shabako's succession to the Ethiopian
throne in 713, his subsequent move into the Delta, and his harsh
treatment of pro-Assyrian rulers like Bocchoris whom he burned
alive (Manetho, fragments 66-68), Egyptian-Assyrian cooperation
was interrupted.

The Sargonid policy of peaceful relations with the Delta Egyptians, however, remained intact until the end of the Assyrian empire,
even though it was temporarily suspended during the years after the
Ethiopians solidified their hold on Lower Egypt. Assyrian campaigns to Egypt during this Ethiopian period always had expulsion of
the XXVth Dynasty leaders as their goal, rather than Assyrian
occupation of the Nile Valley.

This brings us to the issue of the fourteenth year of Hezekiah,
which in 2 Kings 18:13 and Isa. 36:1 is correlated with the year of
Sennacherib's military action against Judah in what we know was the
year 701. Although this date appears to be one of the most secure
synchronisms for a Judean ruler, we cannot accept its accuracy. The
correlation is the product either of pure editorial calculation or is a
misplaced date that was originally associated with Hezekiah's illness
(see 2 Kings 20:1-11; Isaiah 38). The episode of Hezekiah's sickness
came to be connected in popular tradition with the year of Sennacherib's attack, as Isaiah 36-39 and 2 Kings 18:13-20:21 indicate.
When this was done, the promise to Hezekiah of fifteen additional
years (Isa. 38:5) could have come to be understood as having been
made in his fourteenth year, since he ruled twenty-nine years. Thus
the chronological notation in 2 Kings 18:13 and Isa. 36:1 may have
been purely the product of editorial calculation and synchronization.
On the other hand, the date may have been originally attached to the
story of Hezekiah's illness; when the illness came to be associated
with the invasion of Sennacherib, the chronological reference was
likewise transferred. Because his illness began in his fourteenth year
and he ruled twenty-nine years, it was assumed he was granted fifteen additional years. We follow the second of these alternatives,
which allows a number of events to be correlated, beginning with the
fourteenth year of Hezekiah and his period of illness.

It appears that 2 Kings 18:13 and following, and thus the fourteenth-year reference, were not part of the first edition of the Deuteronomistic History. This material was added in the late exilic or early post-exilic edition of the work. We reconstruct the early history of the literature from Genesis to 2 Kings as follows. The so-called Covenant Code (Exod. 21:1-23:19) was promulgated in 742 or 735 by Ahaz. The JE stratum of the Pentateuch was produced in Judah within a decade and a half of the fall of Samaria. The core of Deuteronomy (chaps. 12-26), sharing some similarities to the preaching of Isaiah, was the document of Hezekiah's reform, promulgated rather late in his reign but probably before 705, most likely at the fall festival of the sabbatical year beginning in Tishri 707 (calculating from the first sabbatical regulations promulgated in the Covenant Code in 742 or 735). During Manasseh's reign, the JE history was edited and extended by Deuteronomistic circles to cover the period from creation through the description of Hezekiah as the ideal king, that is, from Genesis to 2 Kings 18:12. The history's negative portrayal of Ahaz and the misrepresentation of historical events during his reign would indicate a significant gap between the time of Ahaz and the work's production; thus, it probably was not produced until after the death of Hezekiah. Its sharp criticism of the Judean monarchs would indicate that the history was not royally sponsored but was rather the product of an underground movement. This version of the Deuteronomistic History probably did not contain the book of Deuteronomy itself, which received further editorial expansion independently. As we shall see, an early form of the P stratum constituted the law book for Josiah's reform.

The traditions about Hezekiah in 2 Kings 18:13-20:19 were thus developed and shaped apart from the first edition of the Deuteronomistic History and did not reach their final form until the exilic or even post-exilic period, when the second edition of the Deuteronomistic history was produced, incorporating Deuteronomy, the Elijah and Elisha stories and other prophetic narratives, the history of Judah from Hezekiah to the release of Jehoiachin (from 2 Kings 18:13 on), and other supplements (but probably no P material).

Now to return to the issue of Hezekiah's fourteenth year. Although Sennacherib did not invade Judah at that time, a cluster of significant events centered around the fourteenth year of Hezekiah (15 Tishri 714-15 Tishri 713), the year in which he became ill. Three events are relevant for understanding the chronology of Hezekiah's

reign. First, the old Ethiopian king Piye died and was succeeded on
the throne by his aggressive brother, Shabako, who began plans for
an invasion and occupation of the Egyptian Delta. Second,
Merodach-baladan, who had seized the throne of Babylon in Nisan
721, shortly after the death of Shalmaneser (*ABC* 73), began an
aggressive counteroffensive against the Assyrians. In a broken fragment, the Babylonian Chronicles notes: "The tenth year [712-711]:
Merodach-baladan ravaged. . . . . . and plundered it" (*ABC* 75). Thus
the Babylonian king was clearly on the offensive by 712. Sargon
described the situation this way:

> Merodach-baladan, son of Iakin, king of Chaldea, seed of a
> murderer, prop of a wicked devil, who did not fear the lord of
> lords, put his trust in the Bitter Sea, with its tossing waves,
> violated the oath of the great gods and withheld his gifts.
> Humbanigash, the Elamite [here Sargon's scribes err since
> this ruler had died in 717; see *ABC* 74], he brought to his aid
> and all of the Sutu, desert folk, he caused to revolt against
> me; he prepared for battle and made straight for Sumer and
> Akkad (*ARAB* II § 66).

Third, the Philistine city of Ashdod led a revolt in the west. Sargon
describes the development of the revolt, noting his replacement of
the rebellious king of Ashdod (Azuri) by his brother (Ahimitu), who
was then deposed by the people and replaced by a usurper, Yamani.
The latter led a popularly supported revolt against Assyria during
which the city constructed a special moat or water source and
enlisted the cooperation of Judah, Edom, Moab, and others,
apparently Cypriotes, in the revolt and in an appeal to an Egyptian
pharaoh for help (*ARAB* II §§ 30, 62-63, 193-195; *ANET* 287).
Isaiah 20 describes the prophet's symbolic action during the course
of the Ashdod-led revolt; Isaiah 22 reports Isaiah's preaching concerning Judah's participation in the revolt.

This configuration of evidence suggests the following interpretation of the events surrounding the period of Hezekiah's sickness. The Babylonian king, Merodach-baladan, planning a major
offensive in the east and hoping to create a second front for Sargon,
sent emissaries to the west (2 Kings 20:12; Isa. 39:1), probably in
714/713 when Sargon was in Urartu fighting King Rusa I (734-714).
Hezekiah, ill and probably confined and thus out of reach of Isaiah

(Isaiah 20), had been forced to turn over administration of the state to Shebna his chief of staff (Isa. 22:15). Shebna led Judah's participation in the revolt and in making a joint appeal to Egypt for help, probably in 713. Shabako had just succeeded Piye in Ethiopia, and his assumption of the throne was taken by Syro-Palestinian leaders as a sign of coming Ethiopian dominance over the Delta leaders and an immediate shift to a strong anti-Assyrian program. During the early phase of the revolt, whose planning and preparation must have occupied over two years (see Isa. 20:3), Shebna led his supporters in excavating the Siloam tunnel (Shebna's "tomb"), whose construction Hezekiah had already planned in anticipation of an eventual revolt from Assyria (see Isa. 22:8b-11).

Egyptian/Ethiopian help for the revolt did not materialize. The pharaoh to whom appeal was made, either Bocchoris or Osorkon IV, apparently refused to contribute troops to any anti-Assyrian movement. Before Assyrian troops arrived in the vicinity of Ashdod, in either Sargon's tenth (712-711) or eleventh year (711-710), probably the former, Yamani fled to Egypt (*ANET* 286; *ARAB* II § 62) and then to the border of Ethiopia (*ANET* 285; *ARAB* II § 79) but received no assistance from either the Delta princes or Shabako. In fact, the Ethiopian ruler returned Yamani to Sargon, bound in chains (*ARAB* II § 80; *ANET* 285). Shabako at the time was preparing to invade the Delta or had already begun his invasion and probably felt he should not encourage troubles with Assyria at the moment.

Sargon's campaign against the Ashdod-led coalition occurred prior to his campaign against Babylon (*ARAB* II §§ 30, 62-63), which took place in his and Merodach-baladan's twelfth year (*ARAB* II §§ 30-37; *ABC* 75; Isaiah 21).

The western rebels appear to have offered weak resistance. Gath and Ashdod were taken. Judah's military leadership apparently fled the field after initial encounters went against them. Isaiah describes the Assyrian attack on Judah in 22:1-7, looking back on the situation after Hezekiah had reassumed leadership and partially reordered his cabinet (Isa. 22:15-25). For Isaiah, the tragedy of the revolt against Assyria was the fact that Judah, in participating, had lost its favored status with Assyria (Isa. 22:8a) and would now have Assyrian forces garrisoned in Jerusalem.

The chronology of the events surrounding Hezekiah's illness, then, is as follows. In 714-713, he became ill and allowed his officials to take over administration of state affairs. By 713-712, Judah was drawn into the western revolt through Babylonian influence, Philistine pressure, and expectations of Ethiopian participation. The digging of the Siloam Tunnel was probably begun early in this period. In either 712 or 711, the Assyrians suppressed the revolt, with Hezekiah recovering from his illness either during the campaign (see Isa. 38:5-6) or shortly after its conclusion. From Sargon's eleventh year (711-710), Jerusalem and Judah, along with all of southwestern Syria-Palestine, were placed under closer supervision by the Assyrians. Sargon actually claims to have provincialized Gath and Ashdod (*ARAB* II § 62; *ANET* 286), but since later native rulers for Ashdod are mentioned it appears that Sargon appointed an Assyrian administrator alongside local rulers. An Assyrian citadel was for the first time established in Jerusalem to supervise Judean administration.

One further correlation can be made between biblical literature and Assyrian history during Sargon's reign. Isaiah's oracle on Tyre in Isaiah 23 reflects conditions produced by the events of 710 and 709. After forcing Merodach-baladan to flee Babylon, Sargon assumed Babylonian kingship in 710 (*ABC* 75). Shortly thereafter, leaders on Cyprus and King Midas of Phrygia, the most powerful ruler in Anatolia, submitted to Assyrian authority (*ARAB* II §§ 70-71, 180-89; *ANET* 284; Postgate 22-25). Such changes in policy were all to the disadvantage of Tyre's freewheeling commercialism and of the Ethiopians in Egypt dependent on Tyrian shipping. For the moment, Sargon had quieted Tyre (*ARAB* II § 118).

In the late spring or early summer of 705, Sargon died on the battlefield. The last entry on him in an eponym list reports: "The king [against Tabal. . . . .] against Eshpai the Kulummaean. . . . . The king was killed. The camp of the king of Assyria [was taken. . . . .]." With his death, revolt was widespread. Hezekiah, now with Isaiah's support, took the lead in the rebellion of southern Syria-Palestine.

Unfortunately, it is impossible to establish with certainty any chronological points in the period of Hezekiah's revolt prior to Sennacherib's western campaign in his fourth year (701-700). We assume that Hezekiah's reforms and nationalistic policies were formulated, if not initiated, before the revolt began. These involved the effort to centralize worship in Jerusalem, the closing of outlying sanctuaries, and the plans for reestablishment of a greater Israel. All were supported by the deuteronomic legislation. The beginning of the sabbatical year 707-706 was probably the time when these steps were inaugurated (see 2 Kings 18:4-8; 18:22; Isa. 27:9).

Isaiah 24-27 was composed for use in the celebration of Judah's declaration of independence from Assyria, the outbreak of the revolt, and the destruction of the Assyrian citadel in Jerusalem. Since Sargon died early in his seventeenth year (Sennacherib assumed the throne on 12 Ab), the revolt may have been fully underway by the new year festival in Tishri 705; this was the occasion of great celebration.

After extensive campaigning in the east, Sennacherib arrived in the west in 701. In spite of several Assyrian texts describing the campaign (see *AS* 29-34, 60-61; *ANET* 287-88; *ARAB* II §§ 239-40, 309-312, 347) as well as biblical descriptions (2 Kings 18:13-19:37; Isaiah 36-37), the course of his actions against Jerusalem cannot be reconstructed in detail. The evidence would indicate the following. Moving down the Mediterranean coast, Sennacherib defeated Phoenician forces under King Luli. Towns controlled by Sidka king of Ashkelon were captured and Sidka himself was surrendered to Sennacherib by his own subjects. While attacking Ekron, Sennacherib was confronted with a combined force of Ethiopian and Egyptian troops, sent into the field by Shabako, perhaps under the command of Tirhakah (2 Kings 19:9). The Egyptians engaged the Assyrians in the neighborhood of Eltekeh and were defeated. Sennacherib resumed actions against Ekron and Judean cities in the Shephelah. He claims to have captured forty-six Judean towns. After preliminary negotiations with the Assyrian Rabshakeh, and with Assyrian preparations underway to lay siege to Jerusalem, Hezekiah submitted to Sennacherib, released King Padi of Ekron whom he held prisoner in Jerusalem, and agreed to accept Assyrian terms of surrender which included a reduction of Judean territory. Hezekiah was allowed to retain the throne; his son and heir, Manasseh, was only ten years old at the time. After establishing order in the region, Sennacherib left the area quickly, probably to handle matters in Babylon where the puppet king Bel-ibni had revolted (*ABC* 77). Hezekiah's payment of tribute was later sent to Sennacherib in Nineveh.

Isaiah seems to have opposed any form of surrender to Sennacherib, arguing that Jerusalem would be divinely saved and that its citizens and the refugees it harbored would form the remnant growth for a rebirth of the people (Isa. 37:30-32). The prophet's somewhat enigmatic remarks in 37:30 indicate that 700-699, "the second year," was a sabbatical year.

Hezekiah died soon after submitting to Sennacherib, after 15 Tishri 699, and was succeeded by his twelve-year old son, Manasseh, who reigned for fifty-five years, dying after 15 Tishri 644 (2 Kings 21:1). Very few correlations can be made between Manasseh's reign and general near eastern history. Sennacherib conducted no further campaigns in Syria-Palestine. He was murdered by one of his sons on 20 Tebet in the twenty-fourth year of his reign (*ABC* 81). The crown prince Esarhaddon entered Nineveh and secured the throne on 8 Adar 680, after a short struggle to suppress his opponents (*ANET* 289-90; *ABC* 81).

In the second year of his reign (679-678), Esarhaddon campaigned in the west, penetrating to the border of Egypt where he destroyed the city of Arsa at the Brook of Egypt and deported its ruler (*ARAB* II §§ 550, 710; *ANET* 290, 303; *ABC* 125). He was back in the west in 677-676 to suppress a revolt in Sidon (*ABC* 83, 126; *ANET* 303). The Sidonian king, Abdimilkutte, was captured and decapitated (*ANET* 303; 290-91; *ABC* 83, 126; *ARAB* II § 527). Sidon's revolt had probably been encouraged by the Ethiopian ruler Tirhakah (690-664) who sought to encourage insurrection in Syria-Palestine throughout his career (see *AGS* II ## 69-70, 109; *IAKA* § 67; *BA* 29[1966]100).

The only explicit reference to Manasseh in Esarhaddon's inscriptions occurs in a listing of the twelve kings of the seacoast and the ten kings from Cyprus forced to assist the Assyrian monarch in transporting building materials from the west to his capital at Nineveh (*ANET* 291). No date is supplied for this undertaking, but the absence of Sidon in the list of vassal states could imply a date after 677, when Esarhaddon claims to have completely destroyed the city.

In his seventh year (674-673), Esarhaddon took drastic action to suppress Ethiopian interference in the eastern Mediterranean seaboard. He invaded Egypt but was defeated there in a bloody battle on 5 Adar and had to retreat (*ABC* 84). In 672-671, he invaded Egypt again, captured Memphis on 22 Tammuz, and took prisoner members of the royal family (*ABC* 85). After his victory, he declared, "All Ethiopians I deported from Egypt--leaving not even one to do homage" (*ANET* 293). On his way to Egypt, Esarhaddon had punished Ba'lu of Tyre and imposed strong strictures on his freedom (*ARAB* II § 710; *ANET* 290-92, 533-34). In describing his rapid journey to Egypt, he mentions Apku (= Aphek) in the region of Samaria (*ANET* 292). In Egypt, Esarhaddon set up a government comprised of non-Ethiopians under Assyrian supervision, thus keeping to the spirit of the cooperative policy between Assyria and Delta Egyptians inaugurated by Sargon after his 720 campaign.

Esarhaddon was compelled in his twelfth year (670-669) to set out for Egypt again where Tirhakah had retaken Memphis and reasserted Ethiopian control over Lower Egypt. The Assyrian king fell sick on the journey and died on 10 Marheshvan (*ABC* 86; *ANET* 303).

In spite of this extensive campaigning through Syria-Palestine and Esarhaddon's settlement of exiles in Samaria (Ezra 4:2), no mention is made of Judah or Manasseh. One event in which Manasseh may have participated was a ceremony in 672-671 at which Esarhaddon concluded vassal treaties with all his subject kingdoms concerning Ashurbanipal's succession to the throne (*ANET* 534-41).

Only a few contacts between Judah and Assyria during Ashurbanipal's long reign (668-627) can be outlined with any confidence whatever. Early in his reign, Ashurbanipal invaded Egypt, again to drive Tirhakah out of Lower Egypt (see *ANET* 294-97 and *ARAB* II §§ 770-83). While pursuing Tirhakah toward Thebes, Ashurbanipal discovered a plot by Delta leaders to support the Ethiopian against him. The plot was suppressed, but Neco I of Sais, who had been involved in the conspiracy, was, after he submitted, elevated to prominence by Ashurbanipal and became the founder of the pro-Assyrian XXVIth Dynasty. Ashurbanipal was forced to invade Egypt for a final time in 664-663 after Tirhakah was succeeded on the Ethiopian throne by his nephew Tantamani (664-656). The latter had again invaded Lower Egypt, and Neco I had died in battle fighting the Ethiopians (Herodotus, *Histories* II 150). Ashurbanipal drove Tantamani and the Ethiopians out of lower Egypt, destroyed Thebes (see Nahum 3:8-10), and elevated Neco's son, Psammetichus I (664-610).

Ashurbanipal's invasions of Egypt provide points of contact with both the history and literature of the Old Testament, in addition to Nahum's reference to the destruction of Thebes. In the so-called Prism A (lines 686-74; see *ANET* 294; *ARAB* II § 771) of his annals, Ashurbanipal mentions being greeted by the vassal kings of the west on his first expedition to Egypt. He reports that he required these

vassals to "accompany my army over the land--as well as over the
sea-route with their armed forces and ships." (Esarhaddon may
already have begun this practice.) The parallel Prism C text offers a
list of these vassals (see *ANET* 294; *ARAB* II § 876) which includes
Manasseh of Judah. Undoubtedly Judeans, if not Manasseh himself,
accompanied Ashurbanipal, and some of these were settled in Egypt
in military garrisons (*Letter of Aristeas* § 13). (Manasseh's successor
was born during the period of Ashurbanipal's Egyptian campaigns
and probably named in honor of the Egyptian god Amon.) The
statement in Deut. 28:68 about returning to Egypt in ships and
dwelling there clearly refers to this episode and probably comes
from a time soon after 664, when the experience was still reasonably
fresh in people's minds. This, plus the similarity of Deuteronomy 5-
6 and 28 to statements in Esarhaddon's vassal treaties of 672-671,
suggests that a second edition of Deuteronomy (chaps. 5-26 + 28)
was produced in the form of a covenant document after this date.

Manasseh died sometime after 15 Tishri 644 and was succeeded
on the throne by his twenty-two year old son Amon (2 Kings 21:17-
19). Amon ruled for only two years before being assassinated by his
courtiers (2 Kings 21:19, 23). The motivation behind the murder of
Amon, the only successful assassination attempt on a reigning
Davidic king, remains a mystery. Whether purely internal family
struggles, domestic party strife, or external international developments played a role cannot be determined. That the "people of the
land" (landowning Judeans or, perhaps, the Judean militia) intervened to kill the assassins and place Josiah on the throne could indicate that a change in state policy was envisioned by the assassins and
their supporters. A widespread revolt against Ashurbanipal overlapped Amon's reign. The most prominent leaders in the revolt
were Arabian tribes and Tyre. The revolt engulfed much of Transjordan and involved Ammon, Moab, and Edom among other states
(*ANET* 297-98; *ARAB* II §§ 817-31). Perhaps the royal assassins
were part of a nationalistic plot to join the anti-Assyrian revolt, but
the movement was suppressed by the "people of the land" who
favored the status quo over such political and military risks.

Josiah succeeded to the throne in 641, in the twenty-eighth year
of Ashurbanipal and the twenty-third year of Psammetichus I. The
early years of Josiah saw increased Egyptian presence in Syria-
Palestine. As allies, Egypt and Assyria probably shared joint rule in
the region for a time. Several factors point to Egyptian involvement

in the region. Herodotus reports that the Egyptians under Psammetichus besieged Ashdod for twenty-nine years (II 157). One could
hypothesize that Herodotus misunderstood and that the city was
taken in Psammetichus's twenty-ninth year, 635. Herodotus also
reports that when "they (the Scythians) were in the part of Syria
called Palestine, Psammetichus king of Egypt met them and per-
suaded them with gifts and prayers to come no farther" (I 105). The
extension of Egyptian authority into Syria-Palestine must have
intensified in the 620s. In 616, the year with which the Babylonian
Chronicles resume after a gap beginning in 623, they note that the
Egyptian army was deep in the heartland of Mesopotamia, and we
must presume was in control of the territory along the *via maris*
throughout the length of the eastern Mediterranean seaboard.

10. FROM THE RISE OF BABYLONIA TO THE
FIRST CAPTURE OF JERUSALEM

JUDAH JOSIAH (641-610)	BABYLONIA NABOPOLASSAR (625-605)
	0. 26 Marheshvan 626 - Nisan 625
17. Tishri 625 - Tishri 624	1. Nisan 625 - Nisan 624
18. Tishri 624 - Nisan 622	2. Nisan 624 - Nisan 623
	3. Nisan 623 - Nisan 622
19. Nisan 622 - Nisan 621	4. Nisan 622 - Nisan 621
20. Nisan 621 - Nisan 620	5. Nisan 621 - Nisan 620
21. Nisan 620 - Nisan 619	6. Nisan 620 - Nisan 619
22. Nisan 619 - Nisan 618	7. Nisan 619 - Nisan 618
23. Nisan 618 - Nisan 617	8. Nisan 618 - Nisan 617
24. Nisan 617 - Nisan 616	9. Nisan 617 - Nisan 616
25. Nisan 616 - Nisan 615	10. Nisan 616 - Nisan 615
26. Nisan 615 - Nisan 614	11. Nisan 615 - Nisan 614
27. Nisan 614 - Nisan 613	12. Nisan 614 - Nisan 613
28. Nisan 613 - Nisan 612	13. Nisan 613 - Nisan 612
29. Nisan 612 - Nisan 611	14. Nisan 612 - Nisan 611
30. Nisan 611 - Nisan 610	15. Nisan 611 - Nisan 610
31. Nisan 610 -	16. Nisan 610 - Nisan 609

JEHOAHAZ II (3 months)

JEHOIAKIM (608-598)

	17. Nisan 609 - Nisan 608
0. . . . . - Nisan 608	
1. Nisan 608 - Nisan 607	18. Nisan 608 - Nisan 607
2. Nisan 607 - Nisan 606	19. Nisan 607 - Nisan 606
3. Nisan 606 - Nisan 605	20. Nisan 606 - Nisan 605
4. Nisan 605 - Nisan 604	21. Nisan 605 - 8 Ab 605

NEBUCHADREZZAR (604-562)

	0. 1 Elul 605 - Nisan 604
5. Nisan 604 - Nisan 603	1. Nisan 604 - Nisan 603
6. Nisan 603 - Nisan 602	2. Nisan 603 - Nisan 602
7. Nisan 602 - Nisan 601	3. Nisan 602 - Nisan 601
8. Nisan 601 - Nisan 600	4. Nisan 601 - Nisan 600
9. Nisan 600 - Nisan 599	5. Nisan 600 - Nisan 599
10. Nisan 599 - Nisan 598	6. Nisan 599 - Nisan 598
11. Nisan 598 - Kislev 597	7. Nisan 598 - Nisan 597

JEHOIACHIN (3 months)

8. Nisan 597 - Nisan 596

10. From the Rise of Babylonia to the First Capture of Jerusalem

H. Cazelles, "La vie de Jeremie dans son contexte nationale et internationale," *BETL* 54(1981)21-39; H. L. Ginsberg, *The Israelian Heritage of Judaism* (New York: Jewish Theological Seminary of America, 1982)39-83; H. J. Katzenstein, "'Before Pharaoh Conquered Gaza'(Jeremiah XLVII 1)," *VT* 33(1983)249-51; A. Malamat, "The Twilight of Judah: In the Egyptian-Babylonian Maelstrom," *SVT* 28(1975)123-45; Malamat, "The Last Kings of Judah and the Fall of Jerusalem: An Historical-Chronological Study," *IEJ* 18(1968)137-56; Malamat, "Josiah's Bid for Armageddon: The Background of the Judean-Egyptian Encounter in 609 B.C.," *JANES* 5(1973)267-79; J. Milgrom, "The Date of Jeremiah, Chapter 2," *JNES* 14(1955)65-69; R. A. Parker and W. H. Dubberstein, *Babylonian Chronology: 626 BC - AD 75* (Providence: Brown University Press, 1956); B. Porten, "The Identity of King Adon," *BA* 44(1981)36-52; A. Spalinger, "Egypt and Babylonia: A Survey (620-550 BC)," *SAK* 5(1977)228-44; H. Tadmor, "Chronology of the Last Kings of Judah," *JNES* 15(1956)226-30; D. J. Wiseman, *Chronicles of Chaldean Kings (626-556 B.C.) in the British Museum* (London: British Museum, 1956).

Struggles for the throne of Assyria after the death of Ashurbanipal made possible Babylon's assertion of its independence, Nabopolassar's ascension to the throne in Babylon, and his ability to stabilize his rule quickly. The Babylonian Chronicle 2 describes the early activity of Nabopolassar and his takeover of the Babylonian throne on 26 Marheshvan 626 (*ABC* 87-90). With Babylon gradually assuming the role of aggressor and Assyria that of defender, Egyptian involvement in the west increased. Foreign dominance over Judah would have shifted to combined Assyrian-Egyptian control. Jeremiah, who began his prophetic career in the thirteenth year of Josiah (629-628), reflects this situation in chap. 2, where Judah is depicted as serving both masters. A few years later, Judah was clearly an Egyptian vassal. Thus there was no period when Judah enjoyed independence from foreign domination during the reign of Josiah.

In his eighteenth year, begun 15 Tishri 624, Josiah carried out an extensive religious reform (see 2 Kings 22:3-23:23). The evidence suggests two important chronological and calendrical factors about this reform. (1) The beginning of the year was shifted from fall to spring, from Tishri to Nisan. (2) The celebration of Passover/Unleavened Bread was altered so that Passover became a distinct celebration. These two factors need further elucidation.

(1) Evidence for the change of calendar from a year beginning in Tishri to one beginning in Nisan is as follows. (a) A Nisan to Nisan year is presupposed by the narrative of Jeremiah 36, concerned with the fourth and fifth years of Jehoiakim. According to Jer. 36:22, the scroll of Jeremiah was burned by Jehoiakim in the winter palace in the ninth month. This makes sense only with a calendar in which the year begins in the spring. (b) The events surrounding the death of Josiah at Megiddo in 610, the three month reign of Jehoahaz, and the failure to celebrate a coronation in 609 are best explained on the basis of a Nisan to Nisan calendar. (c) The thirtieth-year reference in Ezek. 1:1, which is identical to the fifth year of the exile of Jehoiachin in v. 2 (593), becomes perfectly comprehensible if understood as a reference to the thirtieth year following the inauguration of the new system of reckoning in Nisan 622. (d) All dates and synchronisms in the remainder of 2 Kings and in the books of Jeremiah and Ezekiel are understandable on the basis of a Nisan to Nisan year.

(2) In the earliest descriptions of the celebration of Passover/Unleavened bread in the Covenant Code, JE, and D, the celebration is set at the new moon of Abib (or "milky grain") and lasts seven days (Exod. 13:3-10; 23:15; Deut. 16:1-8). The seven days seem to have constituted a single celebration with the home passover meal being observed on the first day of the festival week and a pilgrimage celebration on the seventh day. The regulations in Deuteronomy differ from those in the other two texts in two important ways. Deuteronomic legislation required that the sacrificial activity associated with the first day of the festival should be performed only at the central sanctuary. This had the effect of making the first day of the celebration into a central gathering or pilgrimage festival. In addition, the seventh day of the festival was declared to be merely a day of solemnity on which no work was to be done. Apparently no seventh-day pilgrimage was involved since the pilgrimage had been shifted to the first day.

According to 2 Kings 23:21-23, Josiah and the law book on which he based his reforms called for a celebration of Passover in a manner totally unprecedented in Israelite and Judean history. These verses speak only of Passover without reference to the associated celebration of Unleavened Bread. 2 Kings 23:21-23 thus provides evidence of the observance of Passover as a separate celebration.

The only stratum of tradition in the Pentateuch which advocates beginning the year in Nisan and observing Passover as a distinct celebration is the priestly stratum. The P regulations in Exod. 12:1-20 (see Lev. 23:4-8) not only agree with what appears to have been enacted by Josiah but also call for such regulations to be implemented. Exod. 12:1-20 is not descriptive but prescriptive, not the summation of old tradition but the advocacy of a new position.

If an edition of the Priestly stratum formed the basis for Josiah's innovations then probably more was involved than merely the change in the calendar and the celebration of Passover as a distinct observance. The old single celebration of Passover/ Unleavened Bread was not only divided so as to create two celebrations where there had previously been only one but also both were moved to mid-Nisan. The separate observance of Passover, presumably on the fourteenth of the month, was held for the first time in Nisan 622 (2 Kings 23:21-23). The fifteenth of Nisan, now the first day of the feast of Unleavened Bread, became "the day of the king," replacing the old observance on 15 Tishri. As such, 15 Nisan became a day of convocation (see Exod. 12:16 and compare Deut. 16:7b). 2 Kings 23:9 indicates that some priests did not go along with Josiah's revisions but instead had observed massoth in its traditional form.

The highlighting of the spring festival naturally decreased the importance of the fall festival with its enthronement of Yahweh and ark procession (see 2 Chron. 35:3). The three-day fall celebration had been extended to seven days in the deuteronomic legislation (Deut. 16:13-15), which included numerous features to win popular support and compensate for the loss of local cultic celebrations (see for example Deut. 14:22-29). (Most of the deuteronomic regulations had been repudiated during the reign of Manasseh, probably with widespread non-Jerusalemite support.) The breakup of the fall festival into three distinct celebrations on the first, tenth, and fifteenth to twenty-second days (see Lev. 23:23-36) may have constituted part of the Josianic reform.

The logical conclusion to be drawn from the above considerations is that the law book given by Hilkiah to Shaphan was some form of the priestly tradition of the Pentateuch. Clearly, Exod. 12:1-20 or something very similar must have formed a part of the book of the torah on which Josiah's reforms were carried out. Presumably, as a covenant document, the law book also included a series of blessings and curses, something comparable to the present form of Leviticus 26.

Although the deuteronomistic coloration of the description of Josiah's reforms in 2 Kings 22:3-23:23 would lead one to assume that Deuteronomy was the law book of Josiah's reformation, this was not the case. The deuteronomic flavoring of the description stems neither from the nature of the law book used in the reformation nor from the nature of the reform, but from the fact that the description was written in deuteronomistic circles.

The following, therefore, is the chronology of the events surrounding Josiah's reformation. Josiah began his eighteenth year on 15 Tishri 624. During the course of the year, the priestly book of the law was made public. Josiah used this book as the basis of his reforms, which were fundamentally religious in nature. The implementation of the new calendar meant that Josiah began his nineteenth year on 15 Nisan 622, the day following the unprecedented observance of the Passover on the fourteenth of Nisan in his eighteenth year (2 Kings 23:23), a year extending from 15 Tishri to 15 Nisan, and thus eighteen months long. Tishri 623 would have been the beginning of a sabbatical year, but this was postponed until Tishri 622 (see below).

The final issue of chronology for the reign of Josiah has to do with his death at Megiddo at the hands of Pharaoh Neco II (2 Kings 23:28-30a). We place this late in 610. Psammetichus I died early in 610 and was replaced on the throne by Neco II (610-595). Late in the summer of 610, Neco II led the Egyptian army into battle against the Babylonians for the first time. This battle occurred in the sixteenth year of Nabopolassar (Nisan 610-Nisan 609). For this year, the Babylonian Chronicles report the following:

> In the month Iyyar the king of Akkad [Nabopolassar] mustered his army and marched to Assyria. From . . . . . until the month Marheshvan he marched victoriously in Assyria. In the month Marheshvan the Ummanmanda, who had come to

help the king of Akkad, put their armies together and
marched to Harran against Ashur-uballit who had ascended
the throne in Assyria. Fear of the enemy overcame Ashur-
uballit and the army of Egypt which had come to help him
and they abandoned the city. . . . . they crossed. The king of
Akkad reached Harran and. . . . . he captured the city. He
carried off the vast booty of the city and the temple. In the
month Adar the king of Akkad left. . . . . (*ABC* 95).

The battle between the Babylonians and Assyrians/Egyptians at
Harran took place sometime between Marheshvan and Adar,
between the eighth and twelfth months of 610-609. On its way to
Harran, the Egyptian army would have traveled up the *via maris*.
The Egyptian army stayed at Harran for a time but apparently with-
drew before the assault by Nabopolassar in Marheshvan or Kislev.
Pharaoh Neco set up headquarters in Riblah near Hamath (2 Kings
23:33) and probably did not return to Egypt until after the major
battle the following year (609-608), the seventeenth year of
Nabopolassar. In that year, the Assyrians and Egyptians attacked
Harran and fought against it from Tammuz until Elul, from the
fourth until the sixth month (*ABC* 96).

The evidence of the Babylonian Chronicles and 2 Kings 23:29b-
35 suggests the following chronology for the complex of events surrounding the death of Josiah. Pharaoh Neco marched north through
Palestine sometime before the month of Marheshvan, in late summer or early fall of 610. At this time, for reasons and under circumstances that remain unknown, he killed Josiah at Megiddo. Pharaoh
Neco then moved north to aid his Assyrian allies. The Judeans
returned Josiah's body to Jerusalem, where he was buried, and
placed his son Jehoahaz II on the throne. Neco stayed at Harran for
only a short time before withdrawing across the Euphrates where he
set up camp for the winter at Riblah. Hearing of the placement of
Jehoahaz II on the throne in Jerusalem, he sent and had him
arrested and brought to Riblah. He imposed a fine of one hundred
talents of silver and a talent of gold on Judah for acting without con-
sulting him.

Jehoahaz II was imprisoned at Riblah after having reigned for
only three months. He was held at Riblah until the pharaoh
returned south on his way home after the battle of Harran in the
summer of 609. At that time, Neco designated Eliakim, another son

of Josiah, to reign in Jerusalem; Eliakim took the throne name Jehoiakim. Thus, no king was on the throne in Jerusalem after Neco arrested and deposed Jehoahaz II, probably in Tebet or Shebat 610-609, until after Elul 609-608, and there was no coronation or anniversary of a coronation in Nisan 609. The year was unassigned to any king. Jehoiakim's accession year extended from his appointment by Neco until 15 Nisan 608. His first regnal year was 608-607.

The dates in the book of Jeremiah relating to the reign of Jehoiakim can be established with reasonable certainty. The earliest dated speech is his temple sermon in chap. 26. According to 26:1 this was preached in the accession year ("the beginning of the reign") of Jehoiakim, that is, between Elul 609 and Nisan 608, probably at the fall festival in Tishri 609. His speech on Egypt in 46:3-12 is dated to the fourth year of Jehoiakim (605-604), the year of the battle of Carchemish (46:2), Nabopolassar's twenty-first (and final) and Nebuchadrezzar's accession year. The Egyptian army was defeated first at Carchemish and then in the district of Hamath. The battles occurred in the summer of 605, before 8 Ab, when Nabopolassar died and Nebuchadrezzar returned home, ascending the throne on 1 Elul (*ABC* 99-100). Three chronological references are given in Jer. 25:1-3, namely, the fourth year of Jehoiakim, the beginning (accession) year of Nebuchadrezzar, and the twenty-third year of Jeremiah's preaching (counting from and including the thirteenth year of Josiah). All of these denote the year 605-604. The thirteenth year of Josiah, the time of Jeremiah's call (Jer. 1:2), was 629-628. Normally a calculation of twenty-three years later would give 606-605. The reference in Jer. 25:3 is based on calculating nineteen regnal years during Josiah's reign, including the thirteenth year when Jeremiah began to prophesy (from 629-628 until 610-609), plus four regnal years of Jehoiakim (from 608-607 until 605-604). This makes sense only if the year 609-608 was unassigned to any king and goes uncalculated in the Jeremianic dating. In this same year, the fourth of Jehoiakim, Jeremiah dictated a scroll of his oracles to Baruch (Jer. 36:1).

In Jehoiakim's fifth year (604-603), a special fast was held in Jerusalem in the ninth month (Kislev; Jer. 36:9). This was the first regnal year of Nebuchadrezzar about which we are told:

> In the month Sivan he mustered his army and marched to
> Hattu. Until the month Kislev he marched about victoriously

in Hattu. All the kings of Hattu came into his presence and he received their vast tribute. He marched to Ashkelon and in the month Kislev he captured it, seized its king, plundered and sacked it. He turned the city into a ruin heap. In the month Shebat he marched away and returned to Babylon (*ABC* 100).

Jehoiakim was no doubt one of the kings who submitted to Nebuchadrezzar, probably between Kislev and Shebat of his fourth year, that is, in the late winter of 603 (2 Kings 24:1).

Jehoiakim was a submissive Babylonian vassal for only three years (604-603, 603-602, 602-601). In Nebuchadrezzar's fourth year (601-600), and exactly three years to the month after the fall of Ashkelon (probably the time of Jehoiakim's capitulation), he attacked Egypt.

In the month Kislev he took his army's lead and marched to Egypt. When the king of Egypt heard he mustered his army. They fought one another in the battlefield and both sides suffered severe losses. The king of Akkad and his army turned and went back to Babylon (*ABC* 101).

Jeremiah's speech in 46:13-28, which anticipated a Babylonian victory that never occurred, probably belongs to this period. Apparently, Pharaoh Neco followed up his victory over the Babylonians with a short campaign into Philistia, at which time he took Gaza (see Herodotus II 159). Jeremiah's Philistine speech in chap. 47 was delivered at the time of the Egyptian counterattack. With the tide appearing to turn against Nebuchadrezzar, Jehoiakim withheld tribute (2 Kings 24:1b).

Nebuchadrezzar spent his fifth year (600-599) at home rebuilding his military. In his sixth year (599-598),

In the month Kislev the king of Akkad mustered his army and marched to Hattu. He despatched his army from Hattu and they went off to the desert. They plundered extensively the possessions, animals, and gods of the numerous Arabs. In the month of Adar the king went home (*ABC* 101).

Jeremiah's speech in 49:28-33 stems from this period.

Late in his seventh year, Nebuchadrezzar's forces took Jerusalem, on the second of Adar (16 March 597): "He encamped against the city of Judah and on the second day of the month Adar he captured the city and seized its king" (*ABC* 102). The king at the time was Jehoiachin, whose reign of three months (2 Kings 24:8) or three months and ten days (2 Chron. 36:9) included Tebet, Shebat, and Adar of the eleventh year of Jehoiakim, who died waiting for the Egyptians to arrive and rescue Jerusalem (2 Kings 24:6-7). (The length of Jehoiachin's reign given in 2 Chron. 36:9 reflects the practice of intercalating ten days at the end of a year of twelve lunar months to bring the lunar year into conformity with the solar year.)

According to 2 Kings 24:12b, Jehoiachin was taken to Babylon in the eighth year of Nebuchadrezzar (597-596). Judeans and war booty were also taken from Jerusalem (2 Kings 24:14-16). The context would imply that all of this occurred in the eighth year of Nebuchadrezzar. Jer. 52:28b, however, states that 3,023 Judeans were exiled in Nebuchadrezzar's seventh year. One would assume that after the Babylonian capture of Jerusalem early in Adar Nebuchadrezzar would have returned to Babylon for the celebration of the Akitu/new year festival the first eleven days of Nisan, that is, before the commencement of his eighth year. His return to Babylon would have been a natural time for exiling Judeans. 2 Chron. 36:10 reports that "at the turn of the year" Nebuchadrezzar sent and brought Jehoaichin to Babylon along with the temple treasures and at that time designated Mattaniah as the new king. It is uncertain what "the turn of the year" refers to, whether the intercalated ten days at the end of a lunar year, the period between the beginning of Nisan and the new year celebration, the new year period itself, or merely the beginning of the next year. At any rate, 2 Chron. 36:10, like 2 Kings 24:12b ("and the king of Babylon took him away in the eighth year of his reign"), has Nebuchadrezzar exiling Jehoiachin after the beginning of his eighth year, which commenced at the Akitu festival in Nisan. Jer. 52:28b is probably correct in assigning the exile of at least some Judeans to the seventh year of Nebuchadrezzar. These were probably brought back to Babylon by Nebuchadrezzar when he returned before the beginning of Nisan.

11. ZEDEKIAH AND GEDALIAH

	JUDAH		BABYLONIA
	ZEDEKIAH (596-586)		NEBUCHADREZZAR (604-562)

	JUDAH — ZEDEKIAH (596-586)		BABYLONIA — NEBUCHADREZZAR (604-562)
0.	. . . . - Nisan 596	8.	Nisan 597 - Nisan 596
1.	Nisan 596 - Nisan 595	9.	Nisan 596 - Nisan 595
2.	Nisan 595 - Nisan 594	10.	Nisan 595 - Nisan 594
3.	Nisan 594 - Nisan 593	11.	Nisan 594 - Nisan 593
4.	Nisan 593 - Nisan 592	12.	Nisan 593 - Nisan 592
5.	Nisan 592 - Nisan 591	13.	Nisan 592 - Nisan 591
6.	Nisan 591 - Nisan 590	14.	Nisan 591 - Nisan 590
7.	Nisan 590 - Nisan 589	15.	Nisan 590 - Nisan 589
8.	Nisan 589 - Nisan 588	16.	Nisan 589 - Nisan 588
9.	Nisan 588 - Nisan 587	17.	Nisan 588 - Nisan 587
10.	Nisan 587 - Nisan 586	18.	Nisan 587 - Nisan 586
11.	Nisan 586 -	19.	Nisan 586 - Nisan 585

GEDALIAH (585-582)

0.	. . . . - Nisan 585		
1.	Nisan 585 - Nisan 584	20.	Nisan 585 - Nisan 584
2.	Nisan 584 - Nisan 583	21.	Nisan 584 - Nisan 583
3.	Nisan 583 - Nisan 582	22.	Nisan 583 - Nisan 582
4.	Nisan 582 -	23.	Nisan 582 - Nisan 581

11. Zedekiah and Gedaliah

H. Cazelles, "587 ou 586?," *The Word of the Lord Shall Go Forth* (ed. C. L. Meyers and M. O'Connor; Winona Lake, IN: Eisenbrauns, 1983)427-35; K. S. **Freedy** and D. B. **Redford**, "The Dates in Ezekiel in Relation to Biblical, Babylonian, and Egyptian Sources," *JAOS* 90(1970)462-85; E. **Kutsch**, "Das Jahr des Katastrophe: 587 v. Chr.," *Biblica* 55(1974)520-45; **Kutsch**, *Die chronologischen Daten des Ezechielbuches* (Freiburg: Universitätsverlag, 1985); N. M. **Sarna**, "Zedekiah's Emancipation of Slaves and the Sabbatical Year," *AOAT* 22(1973)143-49; **Sarna**, "The Abortive Insurrection in Zedekiah's Day (Jer 27-29)," *EI* 14(1978)89*-96*; C. **Schedl**, "Nochmals das Jahr der Zerstörung Jerusalems: 587 oder 586 v. Chr.," *ZAW* 74(1962)209-13.

Although Nebuchadrezzar and his troops had captured Jerusalem on 2 Adar, in the twelfth month of his seventh year, matters in Jerusalem were not settled until after the beginning of his eighth year (2 Kings 24:12b). Jehoiachin had surrendered voluntarily (2 Kings 24:12a), but the Babylonians' looted the temple and royal treasuries and determined the deportees. After returning to Babylon, "at the turn of the year" (2 Chron. 36:10), Nebuchadrezzar appointed "a king of his own choice" (*ABC* 102), Jehoiachin's uncle Mattaniah, who took the throne name Zedekiah (2 Kings 24:17). Nebuchadrezzar's return to Babylon before the exile of Jehoiachin and the placement of Mattaniah on the throne allowed the new year to pass in Jerusalem with no Judean monarch on the throne.

Zedekiah's accession year extended from the time of his appointment by Nebuchadrezzar, sometime after 15 Nisan 597, until 15 Nisan 596. Thus 597-596 was not counted as any Judean king's regnal year. Two texts in Jeremiah refer to events during this accession year of Zedekiah. Jeremiah 27 reports on a gathering of national representatives in Jerusalem from Edom, Moab, Ammon, Tyre, and Sidon to discuss rebellion against Babylonia, and notes Jeremiah's proclamation at the time. (Perhaps Jer. 48:1-49:27 dates from this time.) Similarly, Jer. 28:1 concerns the same event and the prophet's controversy with Hananiah over the possibility of success

for the planned revolt. In 28:1, Jeremiah dates the denunciation of
Hananiah in terms of two reference points in order to specify the
exact time the prediction was made. The first reference is to the
accession year of Zedekiah. The second reference pinpoints the
controversy and Jeremiah's prediction of Hananiah's death "in the
fifth month of the fourth year." This later reference denotes the fifth
month of the fourth year of a sabbatical cycle. The year 622-621 was
a sabbatical year, as were 615-614, 608-607, and 601-600. The fourth
year of the cycle begun in Tishri 600, when the last sabbatical year
ended, would have been 597-596, the accession year of Zedekiah.
(The reformation in Josiah's eighteenth year postponed the sabbatical cycle by one year, but even with the change in the calendar sabbatical years themselves continued to be observed from Tishri to
Tishri since plowing and sowing were fall activities.) The fifth month
of a sabbatical year would have been Shebat. Thus the conclave of
potentially rebellious states, and Jeremiah's controversy with
Hananiah, occurred in 597-596, the latter in January/February 596.

The revolt which the ambassadors in Jerusalem were discussing
in Zedekiah's accession year and the eighth year of Nebuchadrezzar
(597-596) was apparently backed in the east by Elam. Jeremiah
denounced this eastern power at the time (Jer. 49:34-39). According
to Hananiah's prediction, the revolt was planned for the ninth or
tenth year of Nebuchadrezzar's rule (Jer. 28:3). The Babylonian
Chronicles note that war with Elam occurred in Nebuchadrezzar's
ninth year (596-595) and that in his tenth year (595-594), "from the
month Kislev until the month Tebet there was a rebellion in Akkad"
(*ABC* 102; see Jeremiah 29, especially vv. 8-9).

In Zedekiah's fourth year and Nebuchadrezzar's twelfth year
(593-592), Zedekiah had to journey to Babylon (Jer. 51:59), perhaps
to explain his policies regarding recent troubles in the west.
Although the Babylonian Chronicles are broken at this point, the
entry for the eleventh year of Nebuchadrezzar notes that "in the
month Kislev the king of Akkad mustered his army and marched to
Hattu" (*ABC* 102), indicating trouble in the west. Jeremiah took the
occasion of Zedekiah's visit to Babylon to send along a scroll of
speeches announcing Babylon's ultimate demise (Jer. 51:59-64; see
50:1-51:58).

Ezekiel received his call to be a prophet in the same year that
Zedekiah visited Babylon (Ezek. 1:2). Dating by the years of
Jehoiachin's exile, the call took place on the fifth day of the fourth

month of the fifth year of the exile. Counting from Nisan 597, this would have been 5 Tammuz (about July 593).

Ezekiel's vision in chapter 8 is dated to the fifth day of the sixth month of the sixth year of the exile (5 Elul or about September 592). We know from Egyptian sources (Rylands IX papyrus; see *CDP* II 64-65) that Pharaoh Psammetichus II (595-589) traveled through Palestine and Phoenicia in his fourth year (592-591). This mission and perhaps a visit to Jerusalem and worship in the temple form the background to Ezekiel's "vision" in chap. 8. The visit also must have greatly impressed Zedekiah, who shortly thereafter withheld Babylonian tribute. Ezekiel's consultation with the elders in Ezekiel 20--on the tenth of Ab in the seventh year of exile, or about August 591--probably occurred near the time of Zedekiah's withholding of tribute.

Babylonian troops did not lay Jerusalem under siege until 10 Tebet in Zedekiah's ninth year (588-587), or about January 587 (2 Kings 25:1; Jer. 39:1). Ezekiel, on 12 Tebet of the tenth year of the exile (588-587) or about January 587, denounced Egypt and any reliance on that nation's help (Ezek. 29:1-16). On two additional occasions, on 7 Nisan in the eleventh year of captivity (about April 587) and on 1 Sivan in the same year (about June 587), Ezekiel denounced Egypt (Ezek. 30:20-31:18).

In Zedekiah's tenth year and Nebuchadrezzar's eighteenth year (587-586), the Egyptians under Pharaoh Hophra/Apries (589-570) did send an expedition into Palestine forcing the Babylonians to raise the siege of Jerusalem temporarily (Jer. 37:5; 32:1-2). Perhaps at this time some 832 persons from Jerusalem were sent into exile by Nebuchadrezzar (Jer. 52:29). With the defeat or withdrawal of the Egyptian army, the siege of Jerusalem was renewed. Because 587-586 was a sabbatical year, the temporary freeing of the Hebrew slaves, which Jeremiah discusses in conjunction with the siege of Jerusalem, probably occurred in Tishri 587, the beginning of the sabbatical year (Jer. 34:8-22). If so, this suggests that the siege of Jerusalem as well as of Lachish and Azekah had resumed by Tishri 587 (Jer. 34:6-7).

The walls of Jerusalem were breached on 9 Tammuz in Zedekiah's eleventh and Nebuchadrezzar's nineteenth year (586-585) or about mid-July 586 (2 Kings 25:3; Jer. 39:2). On 5 or 10 Ab (see 2 Kings 25:8-9; Jer. 52:12) in Nebuchadrezzar's nineteenth year, Nebuzaradan, the captain of Nebuchadrezzar's bodyguard, arrived in

Jerusalem and burned the city and the temple, about eighteeen months after the city was first placed under siege (*Ant* X 116). Word of the city's destruction reached Ezekiel in exile on 5 Tebet in the twelfth year of exile (586-585), or about January 585.

Nebuchadrezzar appointed Gedaliah as the new leader of the Judean people in the land, but his office is not specified (2 Kings 25:22; Jer. 40:7). A case can be made arguing that Gedaliah was appointed king (not "governor" as in most modern translations) with a new ruling family to replace the Davidic house. At any rate, Gedaliah was soon assassinated by Ishmael, a Davidic claimant aspiring to the throne (2 Kings 25:25; Jer. 41:1). Biblical texts simply place this in the seventh month without reference to a year (2 Kings 25:25; Jer. 41:1). If Jerusalem was burned on the fifth or tenth of the fifth month (2 Kings 25:8; Jer. 52:12), it seems impossible that the events following its fall and the rule of Gedaliah at Mizpah could have occurred within a span of little more than a month (see 2 Kings 25:10-24; Jer. 40:7-16). Probably the death of Gedaliah should be placed in the seventh month of his fourth year and the twenty-third year of Nebuchadrezzar (582-581), when there was a further deportation of Judeans (Jer. 52:30). Josephus reports that in this year, Nebuchadrezzar was again in Syria-Palestine fighting the Moabites and Ammonites (*Ant* X 180-82). It was Baalis king of the Ammonites who had encouraged Ishmael's slaughter of Gedaliah and his family (Jer. 40:14; 41:10).

12. THE IMPLICATIONS OF THE PRESENT STUDY

The chronology proposed in this volume has numerous implications for Old Testament study. Here we will only summarize and highlight some of these in terms of three categories.

(1) In terms of purely historical issues, the following points are worthy of note. (a) The chronological data supplied for the kings following Solomon is reasonably trustworthy. The information supplied does not seem to have been influenced by the overall schematic framework which characterizes the data for the preceding periods. Errors and miscalculations in the data are reasonably few and generally understandable. In other words, the data should be taken seriously but critically. (b) In addition to regnal years, a number of events can be dated with reasonable exactitude. For example, Samaria was founded by Omri between Marheshvan 875 and Marheshvan 874. The city was placed under siege by the Assyrians following Marheshvan 724 and was captured by Shalmaneser V between 15 Marsheshvan 722 and 25 Tebet 721. (c) From Omri to Ahaz, Israel and Judah existed, for all practical purposes, as two kingdoms within a single state. This explains numerous historical features as well as such incidental remarks as references to "the two houses of Israel" (Isa. 8:14) and "the kings of Israel" (Mic. 1:14). In addition, it becomes clear that Judah did not simply secondarily appropriate the name Israel in the period after the fall of Samaria. Judah and Jerusalem survived as the remnant of Israel. (d) Chronological calculations support the view that Jehoram of Israel and Jehoram of Judah were one and the same. (e) The impact of Syrian dominance over Israel and Judah during most of the reign of Hazael and part of that of Ben-hadad his son must be given greater importance in historical reconstruction than has previously been the case. (f) Pekah's reign in Israel, begun as a rival kingdom before or during Marheshvan 750 and widely supported for twenty years, produced civil factions and warfare that tore at the fabric of Israelite life. (g) The reign of Hezekiah spanned a highly significant period of ancient near eastern history and its full importance has seldom been recognized in the reconstruction of Israelite history. Uncertainty about the date of his reign has produced overly cautious treatments of his rule. This in turn has led to an overemphasis on Josiah's rule and to exaggerated portraits of the importance of the latter's reign.

(2) The evidence indicated by our chronological reconstruction has numerous implications for the study of Old Testament liter-

ature and literary history. (a) The change in calendar under Josiah, from a fall to a spring new year, presupposes some form of the priestly rather than the deuteronomic stratum of the Pentateuch. This means that an early edition of P was formulated as a law book in pre-exilic times. Josiah's reformation, notwithstanding over a century of research which has presupposed the theory, was not based on Deuteronomy. Although some form of P must be dated to the last quarter of the seventh century, this does not demand the priority of early P over early D. (b) As a law code, the earliest form of D must still be dated prior to the earliest form of P. The most likely date for the origin and promulgation of D in its earliest form is the latter part of the reign of Hezekiah. During this period, after the fall of Samaria, Judean nationalism was strongly fostered at the Jerusalem court and efforts were made to avoid the disaffection of the Judean population as occurred during Ahaz's reign. D gave expression to both of these concerns. The law of the king in Deut. 17:14-17 prohibits the appeal to Egypt for horses, exactly the action taken by Hoshea and the Israelites in 726-725 (see 2 Kings 17:4; Isa. 30-31). This indicates that the core of Deuteronomy does not predate this time. (c) The correlation of terminology between the covenant sections of Deuteronomy and the vassal treaty of Esarhaddon from 672-671 and the reference to Ashurbanipal's campaign to Egypt in 664 in Deut. 28:68 would indicate that the covenant form of Deuteronomy dates from shortly after this period. This revised form of D represents the first full-blown formulation of Israel's relationship to Yahweh in covenant categories. (Hosea speaks of Yahweh's covenant but in terms of Yahweh as the overseer of a covenant relationship between two other parties.) (d) Our reconstruction of a detailed chronology for the second half of the eighth century makes it possible to relate practically all the speeches of the eighth-century prophets--Hosea, Amos, Isaiah, and Micah--to specific historical contexts.

(3) The assumptions and conclusions about calendar reckoning have numerous implications for the reconstruction of socio-cultic life in ancient Israel and Judah. (a) Clearly, the regnal and calendar year began in the autumn in both Israel and Judah until Josiah's eighteenth year. (b) The significance assigned the autumn festival in recent biblical studies is further substantiated by the role it played in calendar considerations. (c) The central importance of the king in the autumn-new year festival and the cultic life of the people has

been reinforced by our study. (d) The history of Passover must be reconceived. Instead of being two festivals that coalesced, Passover and Unleavened Bread were originally one festival that divided. (e) The abdication of some kings for reasons of purity/uncleanness illustrates the operation of priestly regulations in pre-exilic times.

Month Names in the Jewish Calendar

1.	Nisan	March/April
2.	Iyyar	April/May
3.	Sivan	May/June
4.	Tammuz	June/July
5.	Ab	July/August
6.	Elul	August/September
7.	Tishri	September/October
8.	Marheshvan	October/November
9.	Kislev	November/December
10.	Tebet	December/January
11.	Shebat	January/February
12.	Adar	February/March

CHART OF THE ISRAELITE AND JUDEAN KINGS

JUDAH	ISRAEL

ISRAEL
JEROBOAM I (927-906)

REHOBOAM (926-910)

JUDAH	ISRAEL
0. . . . . - Tishri 926	0. . . . . - Marheshvan 927
1. Tishri 926 - Tishri 925	1. Marheshvan 927 - Marheshvan 926
2. Tishri 925 - Tishri 924	2. Marheshvan 926 - Marheshvan 925
3. Tishri 924 - Tishri 923	3. Marheshvan 925 - Marheshvan 924
4. Tishri 923 - Tishri 922	4. Marheshvan 924 - Marheshvan 923
5. Tishri 922 - Tishri 921	5. Marheshvan 923 - Marheshvan 922
6. Tishri 921 - Tishri 920	6. Marheshvan 922 - Marheshvan 921
7. Tishri 920 - Tishri 919	7. Marheshvan 921 - Marheshvan 920
8. Tishri 919 - Tishri 918	8. Marheshvan 920 - Marheshvan 919
9. Tishri 918 - Tishri 917	9. Marheshvan 919 - Marheshvan 918
10. Tishri 917 - Tishri 916	10. Marheshvan 918 - Marheshvan 917
11. Tishri 916 - Tishri 915	11. Marheshvan 917 - Marheshvan 916
12. Tishri 915 - Tishri 914	12. Marheshvan 916 - Marheshvan 915
13. Tishri 914 - Tishri 913	13. Marheshvan 915 - Marheshvan 914
14. Tishri 913 - Tishri 912	14. Marheshvan 914 - Marheshvan 913
15. Tishri 912 - Tishri 911	15. Marheshvan 913 - Marheshvan 912
16. Tishri 911 - Tishri 910	16. Marheshvan 912 - Marheshvan 911
17. Tishri 910 -	17. Marheshvan 911 - Marheshvan 910
	18. Marheshvan 910 - Marheshvan 909

ABIJAH/ABIJAM (909-907)

JUDAH	ISRAEL
0. . . . . - Tishri 909	
1. Tishri 909 - Tishri 908	19. Marheshvan 909 - Marheshvan 908
2. Tishri 908 - Tishri 907	20. Marheshvan 908 - Marheshvan 907
3. Tishri 907 -	

ASA (906-878[866])

JUDAH	ISRAEL
0. . . . . - Tishri 906	21. Marheshvan 907 - Marheshvan 906
1. Tishri 906 - Tishri 905	22. Marheshvan 906 - . . . .

NADAB (905-904)

JUDAH	ISRAEL
	0. . . . . - Marheshvan 905
2. Tishri 905 - Tishri 904	1. Marheshvan 905 - Marheshvan 904
3. Tishri 904 - Tishri 903	2. Marheshvan 904 - . . . .

			BAASHA (903-882[880])
			0. . . . . - Marheshvan 903
4.	Tishri 903 - Tishri 902		1. Marheshvan 903 - Marheshvan 902
5.	Tishri 902 - Tishri 901		2. Marheshvan 902 - Marheshvan 901
6.	Tishri 901 - Tishri 900		3. Marheshvan 901 - Marheshvan 900
7.	Tishri 900 - Tishri 899		4. Marheshvan 900 - Marheshvan 899
8.	Tishri 899 - Tishri 898		5. Marheshvan 899 - Marheshvan 898
9.	Tishri 898 - Tishri 897		6. Marheshvan 898 - Marheshvan 897
10.	Tishri 897 - Tishri 896		7. Marheshvan 897 - Marheshvan 896
11.	Tishri 896 - Tishri 895		8. Marheshvan 896 - Marheshvan 895
12.	Tishri 895 - Tishri 894		9. Marheshvan 895 - Marheshvan 894
13.	Tishri 894 - Tishri 893		10. Marheshvan 894 - Marheshvan 893
14.	Tishri 893 - Tishri 892		11. Marheshvan 893 - Marheshvan 892
15.	Tishri 892 - Tishri 891		12. Marheshvan 892 - Marheshvan 891
16.	Tishri 891 - Tishri 890		13. Marheshvan 891 - Marheshvan 890
17.	Tishri 890 - Tishri 889		14. Marheshvan 890 - Marheshvan 889
18.	Tishri 889 - Tishri 888		15. Marheshvan 889 - Marheshvan 888
19.	Tishri 888 - Tishri 887		16. Marheshvan 888 - Marheshvan 887
20.	Tishri 887 - Tishri 886		17. Marheshvan 887 - Marheshvan 886
21.	Tishri 886 - Tishri 885		18. Marheshvan 886 - Marheshvan 885
22.	Tishri 885 - Tishri 884		19. Marheshvan 885 - Marheshvan 884
23.	Tishri 884 - Tishri 883		20. Marheshvan 884 - Marheshvan 883
24.	Tishri 883 - Tishri 882		21. Marheshvan 883 - Marheshvan 882
25.	Tishri 882 - Tishri 881		22. Marheshvan 882 - . . . .

			ELAH (881-880)
		(Baasha)	0. . . . . - Marheshvan 881
26.	Tishri 881 - Tishri 880	(23)	1. Marheshvan 881 - Marheshvan 880
27.	Tishri 880 - Tishri 879	(24)	2. Marheshvan 880 - . . . .
			ZIMRI (seven days)

			OMRI (879-869)
			0. . . . . - Marheshvan 879
28.	Tishri 879 - Tishri 878		1. Marheshvan 879 - Marheshvan 878
29.	Tishri 878 -		2. Marheshvan 878 - Marheshvan 877

JEHOSHAPHAT (877-853)			
0. . . . . - Tishri 877		(Asa)	
1. Tishri 877 - Tishri 876		(30)	3. Marheshvan 877 - Marheshvan 876
2. Tishri 876 - Tishri 875		(31)	4. Marheshvan 876 - Marheshvan 875
3. Tishri 875 - Tishri 874		(32)	5. Marheshvan 875 - Marheshvan 874
4. Tishri 874 - Tishri 873		(33)	6. Marheshvan 874 - Marheshvan 873

5.	Tishri 873 - Tishri 872	(34)	
6.	Tishri 872 - Tishri 871	(35)	
7.	Tishri 871 - Tishri 870	(36)	
8.	Tishri 870 - Tishri 869	(37)	
9.	Tishri 869 - Tishri 868	(38)	

7. Marheshvan 873 - Marheshvan 872
8. Marheshvan 872 - Marheshvan 871
9. Marheshvan 871 - Marheshvan 870
10. Marheshvan 870 - Marheshvan 869
11. Marheshvan 869 - . . . .

AHAB (868-854)
0. . . . . - Marheshvan 868
1. Marheshvan 868 - Marheshvan 867
2. Marheshvan 867 - Marheshvan 866
3. Marheshvan 866 - Marheshvan 865
4. Marheshvan 865 - Marheshvan 864
5. Marheshvan 864 - Marheshvan 863
6. Marheshvan 863 - Marheshvan 862
7. Marheshvan 862 - Marheshvan 861
8. Marheshvan 861 - Marheshvan 860
9. Marheshvan 860 - Marheshvan 859
10. Marheshvan 859 - Marheshvan 858
11. Marheshvan 858 - Marheshvan 857
12. Marheshvan 857 - Marheshvan 856
13. Marheshvan 856 - Marheshvan 855
14. Marheshvan 855 - Marheshvan 854
15. Marheshvan 854 - . . . .

10.	Tishri 868 - Tishri 867	(39)
11.	Tishri 867 - Tishri 866	(40)
12.	Tishri 866 - Tishri 865	(41)
13.	Tishri 865 - Tishri 864	
14.	Tishri 864 - Tishri 863	
15.	Tishri 863 - Tishri 862	
16.	Tishri 862 - Tishri 861	
17.	Tishri 861 - Tishri 860	
18.	Tishri 860 - Tishri 859	
19.	Tishri 859 - Tishri 858	
20.	Tishri 858 - Tishri 857	
21.	Tishri 857 - Tishri 856	
22.	Tishri 856 - Tishri 855	
23.	Tishri 855 - Tishri 854	
24.	Tishri 854 - Tishri 853	

AHAZIAH (853-852)
0. . . . . - Marheshvan 853
1. Marheshvan 853 - Marheshvan 852
2. Marheshvan 852 - . . . .

25. Tishri 853 - . . . .
JEHORAM (852-841)
0. . . . . - Tishri 852

1. Tishri 852 - Tishri 851

2. Tishri 851 - Tishri 850
3. Tishri 850 - Tishri 849
4. Tishri 849 - Tishri 848
5. Tishri 848 - Tishri 847
6. Tishri 847 - Tishri 846
7. Tishri 846 - Tishri 845
8. Tishri 845 - . . . .

JEHORAM (851-840)
0. . . . . - Marheshvan 851
1. Marheshvan 851 - Marheshvan 850
2. Marheshvan 850 - Marheshvan 849
3. Marheshvan 849 - Marheshvan 848
4. Marheshvan 848 - Marheshvan 847
5. Marheshvan 847 - Marheshvan 846
6. Marheshvan 846 - Marheshvan 845
7. Marheshvan 845 - Marheshvan 844
8. Marheshvan 844 - Marheshvan 843
9. Marheshvan 843 - Marheshvan 842
10. Marheshvan 842 - Marheshvan 841

AHAZIAH (840)
0. . . . . - Tishri 840
1. Tishri 840 - . . . .
11. Marheshvan 841 - Marheshvan 840
12. Marheshvan 840 - . . . .

ATHALIAH (839-833)
0. . . . . - Tishri 839
1. Tishri 839 - Tishri 838
2. Tishri 838 - Tishri 837
3. Tishri 837 - Tishri 836
4. Tishri 836 - Tishri 835
5. Tishri 835 - Tishri 834
6. Tishri 834 - Tishri 833
7. Tishri 833 - . . . .

JEHU (839-822)
0. . . . . - Marheshvan 839
1. Marheshvan 839 - Marheshvan 838
2. Marheshvan 838 - Marheshvan 837
3. Marheshvan 837 - Marheshvan 836
4. Marheshvan 836 - Marheshvan 835
5. Marheshvan 835 - Marheshvan 834
6. Marheshvan 834 - Marheshvan 833
7. Marheshvan 833 - Marheshvan 832

JEHOASH (832-803[793])
0. . . . . - Tishri 832
1. Tishri 832 - Tishri 831
2. Tishri 831 - Tishri 830
3. Tishri 830 - Tishri 829
4. Tishri 829 - Tishri 828
5. Tishri 828 - Tishri 827
6. Tishri 827 - Tishri 826
7. Tishri 826 - Tishri 825
8. Tishri 825 - Tishri 824
9. Tishri 824 - Tishri 823
10. Tishri 823 - Tishri 822
11. Tishri 822 - Tishri 821

8. Marheshvan 832 - Marheshvan 831
9. Marheshvan 831 - Marheshvan 830
10. Marheshvan 830 - Marheshvan 829
11. Marheshvan 829 - Marheshvan 828
12. Marheshvan 828 - Marheshvan 827
13. Marheshvan 827 - Marheshvan 826
14. Marheshvan 826 - Marheshvan 825
15. Marheshvan 825 - Marheshvan 824
16. Marheshvan 824 - Marheshvan 823
17. Marheshvan 823 - Marheshvan 822
18. Marheshvan 822 - . . . .

JEHOAHAZ (821-805)
0. . . . . - Marheshvan 821
1. Marheshvan 821 - Marheshvan 820
2. Marheshvan 820 - Marheshvan 819
3. Marheshvan 819 - Marheshvan 818
4. Marheshvan 818 - Marheshvan 817
5. Marheshvan 817 - Marheshvan 816
6. Marheshvan 816 - Marheshvan 815
7. Marheshvan 815 - Marheshvan 814
8. Marheshvan 814 - Marheshvan 813
9. Marheshvan 813 - Marheshvan 812
10. Marheshvan 812 - Marheshvan 811
11. Marheshvan 811 - Marheshvan 810
12. Marheshvan 810 - Marheshvan 809

12. Tishri 821 - Tishri 820
13. Tishri 820 - Tishri 819
14. Tishri 819 - Tishri 818
15. Tishri 818 - Tishri 817
16. Tishri 817 - Tishri 816
17. Tishri 816 - Tishri 815
18. Tishri 815 - Tishri 814
19. Tishri 814 - Tishri 813
20. Tishri 813 - Tishri 812
21. Tishri 812 - Tishri 811
22. Tishri 811 - Tishri 810
23. Tishri 810 - Tishri 809

24.	Tishri 809 - Tishri 808		13. Marheshvan 809 - Marheshvan 808
25.	Tishri 808 - Tishri 807		14. Marheshvan 808 - Marheshvan 807
26.	Tishri 807 - Tishri 806		15. Marheshvan 807 - Marheshvan 806
27.	Tishri 806 - Tishri 805		16. Marheshvan 806 - Marheshvan 805
28.	Tishri 805 - Tishri 804		17. Marheshvan 805 - ....

JEHOASH (804-789)

			0. .... - Marheshvan 804
29.	Tishri 804 - Tishri 803		1. Marheshvan 804 - Marheshvan 803
30.	Tishri 803 -		2. Marheshvan 803 - Marheshvan 802

AMAZIAH (802-786[774])

0.	.... - Tishri 802	(Jehoash)	
1.	Tishri 802 - Tishri 801	(31)	3. Marheshvan 802 - Marheshvan 801
2.	Tishri 801 - Tishri 800	(32)	4. Marheshvan 801 - Marheshvan 800
3.	Tishri 800 - Tishri 799	(33)	5. Marheshvan 800 - Marheshvan 799
4.	Tishri 799 - Tishri 798	(34)	6. Marheshvan 799 - Marheshvan 798
5.	Tishri 798 - Tishri 797	(35)	7. Marheshvan 798 - Marheshvan 797
6.	Tishri 797 - Tishri 796	(36)	8. Marheshvan 797 - Marheshvan 796
7.	Tishri 796 - Tishri 795	(37)	9. Marheshvan 796 - Marheshvan 795
8.	Tishri 795 - Tishri 794	(38)	10. Marheshvan 795 - Marheshvan 794
9.	Tishri 794 - Tishri 793	(39)	11. Marheshvan 794 - Marheshvan 793
10.	Tishri 793 - Tishri 792	(40)	12. Marheshvan 793 - Marheshvan 792
11.	Tishri 792 - Tishri 791		13. Marheshvan 792 - Marheshvan 791
12.	Tishri 791 - Tishri 790		14. Marheshvan 791 - Marheshvan 790
13.	Tishri 790 - Tishri 789		15. Marheshvan 790 - Marheshvan 789
14.	Tishri 789 - Tishri 788		16. Marheshvan 789 - ....

JEROBOAM II (788-748)

			0. .... - Marheshvan 788
(15.	Tishri 788 - Tishri 787)		1. Marheshvan 788 - Marheshvan 787
(16.	Tishri 787 - Tishri 786)		2. Marheshvan 787 - Marheshvan 786
(17.	Tishri 786 - ....)		3. Marheshvan 786 - Marheshvan 785

AZARIAH (785-760[734])

0.	.... - Tishri 785	(Amaziah)	
1.	Tishri 785 - Tishri 784	(18)	4. Marheshvan 785 - Marheshvan 784
2.	Tishri 784 - Tishri 783	(19)	5. Marheshvan 784 - Marheshvan 783
3.	Tishri 783 - Tishri 782	(20)	6. Marheshvan 783 - Marheshvan 782
4.	Tishri 782 - Tishri 781	(21)	7. Marheshvan 782 - Marheshvan 781
5.	Tishri 781 - Tishri 780	(22)	8. Marheshvan 781 - Marheshvan 780
6.	Tishri 780 - Tishri 779	(23)	9. Marheshvan 780 - Marheshvan 779

7.	Tishri 779 - Tishri 778	(24)
8.	Tishri 778 - Tishri 777	(25)
9.	Tishri 777 - Tishri 776	(26)
10.	Tishri 776 - Tishri 775	(27)
11.	Tishri 775 - Tishri 774	(28)
12.	Tishri 774 - Tishri 773	(29)
13.	Tishri 773 - Tishri 772	
14.	Tishri 772 - Tishri 771	
15.	Tishri 771 - Tishri 770	
16.	Tishri 770 - Tishri 769	
17.	Tishri 769 - Tishri 768	
18.	Tishri 768 - Tishri 767	
19.	Tishri 767 - Tishri 766	
20.	Tishri 766 - Tishri 765	
21.	Tishri 765 - Tishri 764	
22.	Tishri 764 - Tishri 763	
23.	Tishri 763 - Tishri 762	
24.	Tishri 762 - Tishri 761	
25.	Tishri 761 - Tishri 760	
26.	Tishri 760 -	

10.	Marheshvan 779 - Marheshvan 778
11.	Marheshvan 778 - Marheshvan 777
12.	Marheshvan 777 - Marheshvan 776
13.	Marheshvan 776 - Marheshvan 775
14.	Marheshvan 775 - Marheshvan 774
15.	Marheshvan 774 - Marheshvan 773
16.	Marheshvan 773 - Marheshvan 772
17.	Marheshvan 772 - Marheshvan 771
18.	Marheshvan 771 - Marheshvan 770
19.	Marheshvan 770 - Marheshvan 769
20.	Marheshvan 769 - Marheshvan 768
21.	Marheshvan 768 - Marheshvan 767
22.	Marheshvan 767 - Marheshvan 766
23.	Marheshvan 766 - Marheshvan 765
24.	Marheshvan 765 - Marheshvan 764
25.	Marheshvan 764 - Marheshvan 763
26.	Marheshvan 763 - Marheshvan 762
27.	Marheshvan 762 - Marheshvan 761
28.	Marheshvan 761 - Marheshvan 760
29.	Marheshvan 760 - Marheshvan 759

JOTHAM (759-744)

0.	. . . . - Tishri 759	(Azariah)
1.	Tishri 759 - Tishri 758	(27)
2.	Tishri 758 - Tishri 757	(28)
3.	Tishri 757 - Tishri 756	(29)
4.	Tishri 756 - Tishri 755	(30)
5.	Tishri 755 - Tishri 754	(31)
6.	Tishri 754 - Tishri 753	(32)
7.	Tishri 753 - Tishri 752	(33)
8.	Tishri 752 - Tishri 751	(34)
9.	Tishri 751 - Tishri 750	(35)
10.	Tishri 750 - Tishri 749	(36)
11.	Tishri 749 - Tishri 748	(37)
12.	Tishri 748 - Tishri 747	(38)
13.	Tishri 747 - Tishri 746	(39)

30.	Marheshvan 759 - Marheshvan 758
31.	Marheshvan 758 - Marheshvan 757
32.	Marheshvan 757 - Marheshvan 756
33.	Marheshvan 756 - Marheshvan 755
34.	Marheshvan 755 - Marheshvan 754
35.	Marheshvan 754 - Marheshvan 753
36.	Marheshvan 753 - Marheshvan 752
37.	Marheshvan 752 - Marheshvan 751
38.	Marheshvan 751 - Marheshvan 750
39.	Marheshvan 750 - Marheshvan 749
40.	Marheshvan 749 - Marheshvan 748
41.	Marheshvan 748 - . . . .

ZECHARIAH (6 months)
SHALLUM (1 month)

MENAHEM (746-737)

0.	. . . . - Marheshvan 746
1.	Marheshvan 746 - Marheshvan 745
2.	Marheshvan 745 - Marheshvan 744

14.	Tishri 746 - Tishri 745	(40)
15.	Tishri 745 - Tishri 744	(41)

16.	Tishri 744 -	(42)	3. Marheshvan 744 - Marheshvan 743

JEHOAHAZ I (743-728)

0.	. . . . - Tishri 743		
1.	Tishri 743 - Tishri 742	(43)	4. Marheshvan 743 - Marheshvan 742
2.	Tishri 742 - Tishri 741	(44)	5. Marheshvan 742 - Marheshvan 741
3.	Tishri 741 - Tishri 740	(45)	6. Marheshvan 741 - Marheshvan 740
4.	Tishri 740 - Tishri 739	(46)	7. Marheshvan 740 - Marheshvan 739
5.	Tishri 739 - Tishri 738	(47)	8. Marheshvan 739 - Marheshvan 738
6.	Tishri 738 - Tishri 737	(48)	9. Marheshvan 738 - Marheshvan 737
7.	Tishri 737 - Tishri 736	(49)	10. Marheshvan 737 - . . . .

PEKAHIAH (736-735)

			0. . . . . - Marheshvan 736
8.	Tishri 736 - Tishri 735	(50)	1. Marheshvan 736 - Marheshvan 735
9.	Tishri 735 - Tishri 734	(51)	2. Marheshvan 735 - . . . .

PEKAH (734-731)

			0. . . . . - Marheshvan 734
10.	Tishri 734 - Tishri 733	(52)	1. Marheshvan 734 - Marheshvan 733
11.	Tishri 733 - Tishri 732		2. Marheshvan 733 - Marheshvan 732
12.	Tishri 732 - Tishri 731		3. Marheshvan 732 - Marheshvan 731
13.	Tishri 731 - Tishri 730		4. Marheshvan 731 - . . . .

HOSHEA (730-722)

			0. . . . . - Marheshvan 730
14.	Tishri 730 - Tishri 729		1. Marheshvan 730 - Marheshvan 729
15.	Tishri 729 - Tishri 728		2. Marheshvan 729 - Marheshvan 728
16.	Tishri 728 -		3. Marheshvan 728 - Marheshvan 727

HEZEKIAH (727-699)

0.	. . . . - Tishri 727		
1.	Tishri 727 - Tishri 726		4. Marheshvan 727 - Marheshvan 726
2.	Tishri 726 - Tishri 725		5. Marheshvan 726 - Marheshvan 725
3.	Tishri 725 - Tishri 724		6. Marheshvan 725 - Marheshvan 724
4.	Tishri 724 - Tishri 723		7. Marheshvan 724 - Marheshvan 723
5.	Tishri 723 - Tishri 722		8. Marheshvan 723 - Marheshvan 722
6.	Tishri 722 - Tishri 721		9. Marheshvan 722 - . . . .
7.	Tishri 721 - Tishri 720		
8.	Tishri 720 - Tishri 719		
9.	Tishri 719 - Tishri 718		
10.	Tishri 718 - Tishri 717		

11. Tishri 717 - Tishri 716
12. Tishri 716 - Tishri 715
13. Tishri 715 - Tishri 714
14. Tishri 714 - Tishri 713
15. Tishri 713 - Tishri 712
16. Tishri 712 - Tishri 711
17. Tishri 711 - Tishri 710
18. Tishri 710 - Tishri 709
19. Tishri 709 - Tishri 708
20. Tishri 708 - Tishri 707
21. Tishri 707 - Tishri 706
22. Tishri 706 - Tishri 705
23. Tishri 705 - Tishri 704
24. Tishri 704 - Tishri 703
25. Tishri 703 - Tishri 702
26. Tishri 702 - Tishri 701
27. Tishri 701 - Tishri 700
28. Tishri 700 - Tishri 699
29. Tishri 699 - . . . .

MANASSEH (698-644)

0. . . . . - Tishri 698
1. Tishri 698 - Tishri 697
2. Tishri 697 - Tishri 696
3. Tishri 696 - Tishri 695
4. Tishri 695 - Tishri 694
5. Tishri 694 - Tishri 693
6. Tishri 693 - Tishri 692
7. Tishri 692 - Tishri 691
8. Tishri 691 - Tishri 690
9. Tishri 690 - Tishri 689
10. Tishri 689 - Tishri 688
11. Tishri 688 - Tishri 687
12. Tishri 687 - Tishri 686
13. Tishri 686 - Tishri 685
14. Tishri 685 - Tishri 684
15. Tishri 684 - Tishri 683
16. Tishri 683 - Tishri 682
17. Tishri 682 - Tishri 681
18. Tishri 681 - Tishri 680
19. Tishri 680 - Tishri 679
20. Tishri 679 - Tishri 678

21. Tishri 678 - Tishri 677
22. Tishri 677 - Tishri 676
23. Tishri 676 - Tishri 675
24. Tishri 675 - Tishri 674
25. Tishri 674 - Tishri 673
26. Tishri 673 - Tishri 672
27. Tishri 672 - Tishri 671
28. Tishri 671 - Tishri 670
29. Tishri 670 - Tishri 669
30. Tishri 669 - Tishri 668
31. Tishri 668 - Tishri 667
32. Tishri 667 - Tishri 666
33. Tishri 666 - Tishri 665
34. Tishri 665 - Tishri 664
35. Tishri 664 - Tishri 663
36. Tishri 663 - Tishri 662
37. Tishri 662 - Tishri 661
38. Tishri 661 - Tishri 660
39. Tishri 660 - Tishri 659

40. Tishri 659 - Tishri 658
41. Tishri 658 - Tishri 657
42. Tishri 657 - Tishri 656
43. Tishri 656 - Tishri 655
44. Tishri 655 - Tishri 654
45. Tishri 654 - Tishri 653
46. Tishri 653 - Tishri 652
47. Tishri 652 - Tishri 651
48. Tishri 651 - Tishri 650
49. Tishri 650 - Tishri 649
50. Tishri 649 - Tishri 648
51. Tishri 648 - Tishri 647
52. Tishri 647 - Tishri 646
53. Tishri 646 - Tishri 645
54. Tishri 645 - Tishri 644
55. Tishri 644 - . . . .

AMON (643-642)
0. . . . . - Tishri 643
1. Tishri 643 - Tishri 642
2. Tishri 642 - . . . .

JOSIAH (641-610)

0. . . . . - Tishri 641
1. Tishri 641 - Tishri 640
2. Tishri 640 - Tishri 639
3. Tishri 639 - Tishri 638
4. Tishri 638 - Tishri 637
5. Tishri 637 - Tishri 636
6. Tishri 636 - Tishri 635
7. Tishri 635 - Tishri 634
8. Tishri 634 - Tishri 633
9. Tishri 633 - Tishri 632
10. Tishri 632 - Tishri 631
11. Tishri 631 - Tishri 630
12. Tishri 630 - Tishri 629
13. Tishri 629 - Tishri 628
14. Tishri 628 - Tishri 627
15. Tishri 627 - Tishri 626
16. Tishri 626 - Tishri 625
17. Tishri 625 - Tishri 624
18. Tishri 624 - Nisan 622
19. Nisan 622 - Nisan 621
20. Nisan 621 - Nisan 620
21. Nisan 620 - Nisan 619
22. Nisan 619 - Nisan 618
23. Nisan 618 - Nisan 617
24. Nisan 617 - Nisan 616
25. Nisan 616 - Nisan 615
26. Nisan 615 - Nisan 614
27. Nisan 614 - Nisan 613
28. Nisan 613 - Nisan 612
29. Nisan 612 - Nisan 611
30. Nisan 611 - Nisan 610
31. Nisan 610 - . . . .

JEHOAHAZ II (3 months)

JEHOIAKIM (608-598)

0. . . . . - Nisan 608
1. Nisan 608 - Nisan 607
2. Nisan 607 - Nisan 606

3.	Nisan 606 - Nisan 605
4.	Nisan 605 - Nisan 604
5.	Nisan 604 - Nisan 603
6.	Nisan 603 - Nisan 602
7.	Nisan 602 - Nisan 601
8.	Nisan 601 - Nisan 600
9.	Nisan 600 - Nisan 599
10.	Nisan 599 - Nisan 598
11.	Nisan 598 - Kislev 598

JEHOIACHIN (3 months)

ZEDEKIAH (596-586)

0.	.... - Nisan 596
1.	Nisan 596 - Nisan 595
2.	Nisan 595 - Nisan 594
3.	Nisan 594 - Nisan 593
4.	Nisan 593 - Nisan 592
5.	Nisan 592 - Nisan 591
6.	Nisan 591 - Nisan 590
7.	Nisan 590 - Nisan 589
8.	Nisan 589 - Nisan 588
9.	Nisan 588 - Nisan 587
10.	Nisan 587 - Nisan 586
11.	Nisan 586 - ....

GEDALIAH (585-582)

0.	.... - Nisan 585
1.	Nisan 585 - Nisan 584
2.	Nisan 584 - Nisan 583
3.	Nisan 583 - Nisan 582
4.	Nisan 582 - ....